I0022262

The
Websters' Dictionary

How to Use the Web to Transform the World

By Ralph Benko

SURGEON GENERAL'S WARNING: The Websters' Dictionary is not an actual dictionary. It is the lexicon and instruction manual for those Websters piloting or test-piloting the World Wide Web in the advocacy, policy, and political universes. Unscientific research has proven that reading it can be dangerous to lame websites.

The Websters' Press, Washington,
District of Columbia

Copyright ©2008 by Ralph Benko

ISBN: 978-0-9820756-1-6

Licensed under
a Creative Commons
Attribution-Noncommercial 3.0
United States License.
http://creativecommons.org/licenses/by-nc/3.0/us/

Put it before them briefly so they will read it, clearly so they will appreciate it, picturesquely so they will remember it, and, above all, accurately so they will be guided by its light.

— Joseph Pulitzer

DEDICATION, APPRECIATIONS, AND EXONERATIONS

T HIS BOOK IS DEDICATED TO MY beloved Laura Kuhn, muse, advisor, inspiration, and *la miglior fabbra*; my beautiful and talented children Jessica, Sarah, Michael, and David; and my lovely, soulful brother Stephen and our dear parents Max and Rosalind Benko.

Heartfelt thanks to:

The Searle Freedom Trust, for providing the resources to enable the writing and publication of this work, with special gratitude to the late Dan Searle for having established this Trust as a powerful beacon of freedom and putting it into the hands of the discerning Kim Dennis and its Trustees. The Americans for Tax Reform Foundation for hosting me in the writing, with special appreciation to Chris Butler and Grover Norquist, two great-hearted (and witty) champions of liberty and humanity. Phil Kerpen for his valued support and wise counsel throughout.

Knox Bronson, who taught me much of what's technically accurate in here and nothing that's technically wrong. The giants who created the Internet, on whose shoulders we all stand: Vannevar Bush, Paul Baran, J.C.R. Licklider, Leonard Kleinrock, Bob Taylor, Bob Kahn, Vint Cerf, Larry Roberts, Bob Metcalfe; Tim Berners-Lee, for having invented the World Wide Web; Marc Andreessen for inventing the Web browser. Ray Tomlinson, for having invented the @ sign. And for inventing email. Damn you, Tomlinson.... The Creative Commons people, especially the godfather of Creative Commons, Lawrence Lessig, for this elegant contribution to the culture of the Web and the world to which this book is much indebted. Jimmy Wales and his posse for the Wikipedia. Steve Forbes and George Gilder for their generous words of praise.

The "consultant's consultant," Elsom Eldridge, Jr., www.obvious-expert.com, for inspiring me to share these secrets with the world. Linda J. Parker, my guardian angel who was instrumental in bringing this book to life. Michael Dobson, for his valuable contribution on project management and his early, invaluable, advice on the manuscript. My editor, Bill Cassel for putting this into better English. Paige Ragan, cover artist extraordinaire. Integrative Ink, for composition. Meryl Benko, proofreader extraordinaire. And all those involved with the Landmark Forum for ... Nothing.

My partners at Capital City Partners: Jeffrey Bell, who decisively redefined populism and politics for the 21st Century and for me; Frank Cannon, whose personal integrity and astuteness are a continuing inspiration; Bob Heckman, for those great McCain lapel pins and his continuing service to the Republic.

The wrongheaded opinions and factual mistakes herein are my own darn fault. When you catch me in some stupid mistake, just come on over to TheWebstersDictionary.com's Bar and Grill and set me straight. It'll be fixed in a future edition. (If you're the shy type, write me at RalphBenko@TheWebstersDictionary.com.)

TABLE OF CONTENTS

Table of Contents

INTRODUCTION

http://www.nasaimages.org/luna/servlet/detail/nasaNAS~20~20~120356
~227055:Earthrise---Apollo-8
Failure is not an option.

THIS IS THE DAWNING OF the Age of the Internet.

The World Wide Web is emerging and evolving in (and, from without, into) the nation's capital, Washington, D.C. It is doing so in such interesting ways that even the old mainstream media is noticing—and beginning to grapple with the implications.

But how do you work with the Web from the "supply side"? How do you use the Web effectively, efficiently, and even elegantly to achieve your mission? This remains something of a mystery to most people involved in public affairs. Yet advocacy on the Web is evolving right on track. Its trajectory was foreseen by a very few populist visionaries, men such as Joe Trippi, original Dean presidential campaign manager, who immediately grasped how important it would become to our political well being.

Taking advantage of the power of the Web remains tricky and sometimes appears intimidating. It need not be either.

Backstory: The Trip Through Hell

About two years ago, I, the "Webster," decided to learn how one really goes about using the Web for social transformation, policy, advocacy, and politics. This included learning as much as possible about what goes into designing and publishing websites—such as what, if anything, the great Web advocacy successes have in common; how one finds, evaluates, and hires a capable site developer; what you really can do with—and expect from—a website (really, website doesn't do it justice anymore, it's more like a webvehicle); what success takes and how much—or how little—all this costs.

Moving myself from just one more "unique visitor" to a site publisher made me feel a bit like Dante, lost "within a forest dark."

Midway upon the journey of our life
I found myself within a forest dark,
For the straightforward pathway had been lost.

Ah me! how hard a thing it is to say
What was this forest savage, rough, and stern,
Which in the very thought renews the fear.

(Dante, *Inferno*, translation by Longfellow)

I was confronted with a vast array of resources—articles, books, cryptic statements from techies mysteriously involved with the Web, and, of course, uncountable pieces published on the Web itself.

The information out there was disorganized, required a great deal of piecing together, and often assumed a level of baseline technical knowledge and technique that most people simply do not possess. Danger—at least the danger of failure and of looking foolish—lurked everywhere. It was impossible to find a comprehensible step-by-step guide to what to do (and, perhaps as important, what pitfalls to avoid).

Instead of a roadmap there was a sign at the mouth of the cave of the Web:

ALL HOPE ABANDON, YE WHO ENTER HERE.

The trip through entailed two years of trial and error. That kind of latitude simply is not available to a policymaker, analyst, or institute executive with a real-time mission to fulfill and an image to maintain. That said, the Web is absolutely crucial to any 21st century communications strategy; organizations fail to use it—or fail to use it well—very much at their peril.

If only there were a simple book that explained what a public advocate, nonprofit leader, or policy analyst really needs to know to get it right. A simple book for a non-techie that lays out the basics....

I couldn't find one. So I wrote one. This one.

To belabor the Divine Comedy metaphor just one more time, the Webster designed this book to help you avoid having to harrow Web Hell, to let you skip over Web Purgatory, and send you directly to Web Paradise. (Paradise 1.0 and 2.0. There are plenty of higher circles of Heaven ... so stay tuned for the sequel.)

Of course, a tour through Hell is not without interest. So if you have the time for it... good luck. Send postcards. Or email. But remember, they're still on dialup down there.

Structure of *The Websters' Dictionary*

First, why "Websters"? Because there was no word to describe those of us who are piloting (or even test-piloting), rather than visiting or building, websites or webvehicles. "Webmaster" relates to the technical administration of websites. Those involved in advocacy generally are called "activists." Those involved in policy are lovingly called "wonks." Those involved in politics, "operatives." The Webster offers this new taxonomic category for us activists and wonks and operatives who are determined to turbocharge our effectiveness by using the Web well. (Maybe *Websters* will stick. Maybe not.)

The substantive chapters are organized in step-by-step fashion. If the early chapters cover ground you already feel comfortable with, feel free to skip them. That said, however, there is a certain structure to the dynamic of the Web. By skipping those parts you believe you already grasp, you risk losing some key threads that run throughout.

Chapter 1 provides an overview of the entire process of establishing your presence on the World Wide Web. It begins the process of defining and demystifying the Web for policy, advocacy and political people.

Chapter 2 will provide the reader with a rough idea of how much an organization needs to be willing to spend, what to spend it on, and why.

Chapter 3 gives an overview of the state of play on the Web as this book goes to press. It will begin to be obsolete the moment it is published so you are invited to the companion website www.TheWebstersDictionary.com for breaking developments of interest to the web-based advocacy and policy community.

Chapter 4 looks at the various kinds of tools available—especially those relevant to an advocate or policymaker. Knowing what you can do easily with the Web has relevance to your site's design and structure.

Chapter 5 offers a focused look at some major websites that are relevant to the political, advocacy, and policy communities—and some more minor ones as well. What are the big success stories? Who is behind them? How do they do it? The Web is evolving rapidly but there is no point in reinventing the wheel.

Chapter 6 will tease out some of the implications of lessons learned. What your webvehicle and team look like will be determined by what it is you wish to accomplish.

Chapter 7 addresses some of the basic Web frameworks you have at your disposal in designing your webvehicle.

Chapter 8 addresses the challenging issue of selecting, and managing, a Web designer/developer.

Chapter 9 explains what all this means, or might mean, to an average reader. Even if you are, as surely you are, an above-average reader, it may help you to become a more informed Web user.

Chapter 10 is an interview with a virtuoso Web designer Knox Bronson to give a better appreciation of how it looks from the developer's side.

Chapter 11 lays out the basic aspects of some legal points a site publisher would do well to keep in mind.

Chapter 12, the conclusion, sums up the primary laws of using the Web to transform the world.

Appendix A discusses some very cool websites that were, until the Webster here broke Washington's Code of Silence, semi-secret ways to find out what really is going on without having to use technological antiques called "newspapers" and "magazines" (information delivery systems dating from the 15th century that still show signs of confusion about being Biblical, á la Gutenberg's *Bible*, in authority).

Appendix B is an authoritative study contributed by an expert, Michael Dobson, on the application of fundamental project management principles to creating and operating a webvehicle. For larger, more methodical, organizations it will provide a valuable roadmap to the process. Even for smaller organizations, or an individual, it is valuable to understand clearly the "triple constraints" of a project—time, quality, and budget—and to have a comprehensive overview of all of the steps in the process.

Thank you for taking the time to read this book and to investigate how the World Wide Web can be put to use to get out a message and to build a community. May it prove useful, in the admittedly often clamorous and even sloppy fashion of populism, in helping you guide our officials in the paths of righteousness.

1

AN OVERVIEW OF THE GOOD, THE BAD, AND THE UGLY

http://commons.wikimedia.org/wiki/Image:US_Capitol_Dome_High_R
es_Jan_2006.jpg
Every Webster's Objective: guide them on the paths of righteousness.
(Sometimes known as "fomenting a bloodless coup.")

L ET'S FACE IT: PUTTING UP and managing a website is bewildering. There are many factors contributing to the widespread confusion. The Webster designed this book largely to demystify it for you.

Why is this book necessary? Creating and managing a Web presence is founded in a somewhat mystifying technology. It has its own jargon and uses confusing acronyms like HTML, XML, PHP, and AJAX; and behind the acronyms stands even more incomprehensibility. (Does it help to learn that AJAX is an acronym for *Asynchronous JavaScript and XML*? I didn't think so.)

The mystery is compounded because the technicians and artisans who design, develop, and to some degree manage websites often find it challenging to explain their craft to laypeople. Out of earshot they call us "Earthlings." There's a school of thought that they all come from Area 51 in Roswell, New Mexico. (That would explain a great deal.)

However, unless you want to learn how to do it all yourself—which is not recommended for any but the bravest or most foolhardy adventurers—you're going to have to learn how to communicate with this... different breed. Doing so will require you to understand at least some of the fundamental dynamics of the Web, though not the highly technical stuff. You'll also need to know what exactly you wish to do with the Web, learning what is technically possible. But this demands more time, and more basic geekiness, than most normal people possess. Not, however, more geekiness than the Webster possesses.

Happily, the Webster has put the basics into this book. Thus armed, you will at least know what to be looking for, what questions to ask, and what to expect. This book is designed to be the little cartoon light bulb over your head.

This book lays out fairly succinctly the key points to make it easier to grasp what you can do with the Web today. And what you can do now that you couldn't, as a practical matter, do or afford to do way back in 2006...or even 2007. It will help you grasp what the really powerful elements are now and how you can take advantage of these. Because behind all the jargon it's actually surprisingly simple.

Dealing with technology—and technicians—is only one part of using the Web to transform the world, and in many ways not the most critical part. The greater challenges lie in communicating with the actual human beings who are the intended community for your high-powered webvehicle.

How can you be compelling enough to enroll thousands, or even millions, of people in your cause? How can you forge them into a community and mobilize them to take action?

What kind of webvehicle can easily and inexpensively be managed on a day-to-day basis, while still making your site really compelling to visitors, bringing in crowds, and building a community for them? What part of bringing them in, bonding them to your organization, and educating and mobilizing them will be the responsibility of your dot org and how much of it can come from some kind of Web magic?

The late Sir Arthur C. Clarke once formulated a relevant observation, now known as Clarke's Third Law: "*Any sufficiently advanced technology is indistinguishable from magic.*" That's how many people, even savvy ones, treat the Web—as something magic. It can be magical, but it's not magic. The Web is simply an advanced technology.

Perhaps Clarke's Second Law will prove more pertinent to those who wish to master the Web: "*The only way of discovering the limits of the possible is to venture a little way past them into the impossible.*" Clarke's Second Law is set forth in the final Chapter, along with nine other laws that are key to succeeding on the Web.

Venturing a little way past the limits of the possible need not be daunting. Follow the Webster.

Summary of the Most Important Things to Know

This is a summary of some of the most important factors in using the Web to transform the world. Each chapter provides particulars. Because so much is unfamiliar to the lay reader, however, it might be helpful to have the basic governing principles summarized.

Pulitzer's Law

The fundamental principle of using the Web effectively was stated, paradoxically, by a man who died in 1911, eons before the Internet emerged: Joseph Pulitzer.

It is so important for success that the Webster reiterates it in *The Dictionary* three times: as the epigram, here, and as the first of the ten laws in the last chapter. Pulitzer's Law is far more powerful than dynamite. (Use it only for Good or you will be in violation of The Websters' Oath and subject to expulsion from the Noble Order of Websters.) This is Pulitzer's Law:

Put it before them briefly so they will read it, clearly so they will appreciate it, picturesquely so they will remember it, and, above all, accurately so they will be guided by its light.

This is the fundamental law by which websites live and die. It requires only the following Webster's Corollary to be complete:

And give them easy, simple, direct ways by which their voices may be heard and by which they can, individually and in concert, take action.

A surprising number of people seem to believe that you can just publish a website and thousands of people are bound to flock there. Similar principles to those governing whether a book or magazine finds and engages people apply to publishing on the Web. The Web is just a way of reaching people. Will people find what you have to say easily accessed, interesting, and relevant to their lives?

Before turning to the technicalities, the Webster asks you to ask yourself a threshold question. Investing in Web development is the least costly, least significant aspect of this process. You can get a perfectly serviceable Website for between zero and $20,000 depending on what you intend to do with it and whether you know how to shop for it.

The real expense comes in furnishing it with content, promoting it, and cultivating a devoted community through the medium of the Web. Stick with a very basic website unless you understand that success invariably requires a high-powered team. If you are not prepared to deploy a determined team to succeed on the Web, you don't need a sophisticated webvehicle and you don't need this book. So save yourself some time and just Don't Go There.

Dr. D. Calvin Andrus of the CIA's Directorate of Support, in his now-classic study *Toward a Complex Adaptive Intelligence Community: The Wiki and the Blog*, published by The Center for Intelligence Studies, asserts that *the only way to meet the continuously unpredictable challenges ahead of us is to match them with continuously unpredictable changes of our own.* He goes on to note that ... *a successful virtual community is 90 percent culture and 10 percent technology.*

The Web is magical because it is much, much less expensive than print publishing or buying and operating your own radio or TV station. The Web is magical because it allows your readers to participate. The Web is magical because it allows you to build and mobilize a community.

But the Web is not magic and will not turn lead to gold, no matter how sophisticated your site. You may have a custom-coded dynamic PHP Hypertext Preprocessor framework developed at the cost of many tens of thousands of dollars that can do all sorts of amazing things. But if you don't have people behind it to actually *do* the amazing things, a commitment to it, and a grasp of the basic principles of how to work with it, all that money and hard work will have been invested in vain.

What matters? How interesting, relevant, and visually arresting is your message? How well do you say it? How ardently and deftly do you promote it? How much do you permit your visitors to participate in developing your narrative? Do you really understand bottom-up distribution of power, and community building and mobilization? Are you prepared to go to this new, different, dynamic model?

As scientific savant Carver Mead says, "listen to the technology." There are some things—really, more every month—which you can do with the Web extremely well and affordably. You don't have to use every tool in the kit. In fact, you can succeed by using just one tool very well. Yet there is power in knowing what is in your toolkit.

Power Comes from the People

The dynamism of engaging thousands or millions of people is very different from managing dozens, or even thousands, of employees. And it's also different from just hanging out and chatting (or, on Twitter, tweeting).

As the Chinese sage nicknamed Old Longears, Lao Tzu, once said, "Govern a great state as if you were cooking a very small fish: overhandling ruins it." The open secret here is that the Web's big success stories are based in its inherent populism—its position as giving voice to, rather than talking at, masses of people.

If people wish to simply listen or watch, be passively entertained or informed, they'll watch TV—maybe even C-SPAN—or listen to Rush Limbaugh or NPR. A common denominator for success on the Web—from AOL in its early days to YouTube today—is that it allows people to get their own voices heard (and images seen), from email to blogs to social networking sites to uploaded videos.

From a political and policy perspective, this means creating space for the issues about which your community—and there are many possible communities—is intensely passionate. To borrow from Emma Lazarus: *Unleash the imprisoned lightning.*

This means NOT trying too hard to set an agenda and NOT trying too hard to get people to follow. It is more about using your discernment to sense what your community is enthusiastic about—and which of their enthusiasms you can conscientiously support—and what actions they themselves wish to take, then encouraging and enabling them in this. This means embracing the third axiom of the great sage of democratic organizing, Fred Ross: *An organizer is a leader who does not lead but gets behind the people and pushes.*

MoveOn.org, the greatest success of its kind, got its start as a rallying place created by "Flying Toaster" moguls Joan Blades and Wes Boyd in opposition to the Clinton impeachment. A few years later a young activist named Eli Pariser (now MoveOn's prime operative) got his start with an anti-war petition after 9/11 that spontaneously grew to 500,000 names—and email addresses.

Blades, Boyd, and Pariser then combined lists and transformed MoveOn into an entity that 3.3 million people now trust for guidance on how effectively to act to support their values and worldview. If a dozen organizations from across the political spectrum follow similar practices for their own communities there will be a dozen powerful citizen advocacy networks—and America will be better for it. Many would-be MoveOns pay lip service to the bottom-up model while trying to impose a top-down one that puts the power back at the top and converts their members to minions. Top-down power does not energize people.

After Boyd, Blades, Pariser (and to a lesser extent Zach Exley, a big figure in MoveOn's history, and, by all accounts, a real provocateur and a wit), the next key figure in the history of the Web as powerful advocacy tool is political consultant Joe Trippi. Trippi discovered the Web's power—in the ancient era of 2004. In his loopy humility Trippi might argue that the Web discovered him. He put it into service for Vermont Governor Dean's then quixotic-seeming presidential bid.

In his always fascinating and truly indispensable campaign memoir, *The Revolution Will Not Be Televised,* Trippi makes some perceptive observations about how to manage such a team.

Inside the campaign, we were always looking for ways to show our faith in the people out there, to involve them in what we were doing, to take our cues from them, to model the campaign on their passionate involvement. At one of these meetings with ... our young finance director, we tossed out the idea of posting our fund-raising—not just the results, like other campaigns, but the goal. Invite the people in and open up the books. Give them the knowledge and information—how much money we wanted to raise—and they'd take the responsibility for doing it.

We were in uncharted territory here. No campaign has ever announced the amount of money it hopes to raise.

The next week was the most amazing thing I've ever seen in a campaign." (pp. 130-131)

This could be called "Trippi's Law": *If you pay attention to the community you're building, then the community will step up and do the work.*

Trippi's Law expresses the "how to" beautifully. That grasped, what kind of team will you need to foster such a community. How big should it be? Actually, it begins with one person—the right person—and, if you have initial success, it grows from there. MoveOn typically manages with a team of 16—including in-house technical people— adding a few temporary specialists during heavy seasons such as before election time.

MoveOn doesn't even maintain a central office. Its staff members are widely geographically dispersed. In fact, by internal policy it prohibits even those who reside in the same city from sharing offices.

How amazing is it that fewer than two dozen can organize and mobilize 3+ million? The leadership serves as the "fulcrum" on which the huge lever that is MoveOn's community rests. And in an era of celebrity culture, it is a tribute to the humility and dedication of its leadership that their identities remain so obscure.

As MoveOn approached the 10th anniversary of its founding (September 24th, 1998, only 6 days after the registration of the domain name—that's about how fast you could be moving), it provided its first major journalistic access to journalist Christopher Hayes, who published his extremely striking findings in *The Nation*.

MoveOn pioneered an entire approach to conducting politics through the Internet that has been replicated and spun off across the country and around the globe, an approach that, as the Obama campaign has dramatically demonstrated, has permanently transformed the landscape of American politics.... Before MoveOn pioneered the online petition, just the simple act of gathering 100,000 signatures would have cost hundreds of thousands of dollars and hundreds of hours of labor. Now MoveOn sends out e-mail petitions several times a month. Or consider this: to manage its lobbying efforts and programs for its more than 4 million members, the NRA has a staff exceeding 500 and a $15 million, 390,000-square-foot office building in Virginia. MoveOn has a staff of... twenty-three.... When MoveOn sends out mass e-mails, staffers often first test multiple separate subject lines within small sample groups, choosing the subject that's most effective at getting people to act on the e-mail's "ask." Each week they run a tracking poll, *surveying a random subsample of members to identify which issues they're following and where their passions lie.*

http://www.thenation.com/doc/20080804/hayes

By the evidence, irrespective of uncharacteristic and rare blunders like the ugly "General Betray Us" caper, and whatever you think of MoveOn's politics and policy stands, its leaders are smart, relentless, respectful of their base, witty, and dedicated to winning rather than to self-aggrandizement.

What could be called "Pariser's Law"? *This is not about us, it's about you.* Once again, this represents a cultural shift to a populist ethos where the leaders are sensing, building, and channeling the power of a community. (Surprise! Virtually all successful, constructive mass movements, now as then, are made of this.)

It's a Big World

MoveOn has 3+ million people who can be moved to donate money to candidates and causes, mobilize as grass roots volunteers, contact their elected officials, and act powerfully in concert. Impressive? Most! Evidence has persuaded the Webster that MoveOn imparted the initial, crucial, critical mass to Barack Obama's presidential bid. It previously was crucial to Howard Dean's shocking initial momentum in 2004. And its power is growing.

That said ... 3 million people represents only 1% of America's population. It is equivalent to a city slightly smaller than America's *second* largest city, Los Angeles. Is L.A. influential? Yes. Is L.A.'s voice heard? Loudly! (Some might say a little too loudly.) Does it call the shots for the rest of us? Not even close.

Note, for example, the different roles Web activism played in the Obama campaign before and after he secured the nomination. When Obama was emerging from obscurity, MoveOn and MyBarackObama were able to create a mass movement around him—composed of what Web visionary David Weinberger elegantly dubbed "small pieces loosely joined." This was critical in his initial success at raising large sums of money in small amounts. And in motivating activists to get out there and organize—something especially critical in the caucus-state driven strategy that Obama's campaign strategist David Axelrod and his team shrewdly used to outfox Hillary Clinton.

In the process, MoveOn demonstrated many of the characteristics of a successful insurgency. The laws of guerilla warfare, as summarized in Robert Taber's definitive *War of the Flea*, require that insurgency give way to conventional warfare where mastery of a different set of variables is required to prevail. Thus, the Obama supporters who were mobilized through the Web play a very different role after the nomination than they did before, and, if their candidate prevails, will play a still different role during an administration. Such rules apply both on and off the Web.

In any event, to political professionals, polling at 1% is called asterisk territory.

The number of people who visit MoveOn's homepage each day averages, according to Web ratings site Quantcast.com, around 15,000. (Recently, as things have heated up, traffic has been about twice that; it fluctuates.) *Even 30,000 visitors a day is about 1% of the number of people who visit the most popular sites on the Web. Asterisk territory.*

15,000 reportedly doesn't do justice to MoveOn's traffic, as the traffic they generate from their main engine—email to the community—is brought in to internal pages which do not show up in Quantcast's statistics (which are, in any event, a rough estimate).

And yet these figures, however rough, give a useful context. See how much force even a 1% minority working in concert can exert? This is a valuable example of the power of coherence. A laser and a light bulb both emit photons. The difference between them is that a laser bounces the photons around in something called a nova tube, which causes them to behave coherently. With power to cut through steel.

In Internet terms, MoveOn's traffic is tiny. And yet, how powerful: Under the guidance of the lamalike (as *The Nation* characterized him) Eli Pariser and his exceptionally bright, devoted team, MoveOn can direct millions of dollars to candidates and causes.

This gives this community, the "netroots," a powerful voice, a voice that must be taken into account by officials and candidates, particularly within the Democratic Party. Not loud enough to force even the Democratic Party to stand for the immediate withdrawal of troops from Iraq but a force to be reckoned with. There is no other group, either on the Right or the Left, that's even close in terms of using the Web with mass impact—although there are other important groups using the Web (in a few cases well). More such groups are emerging.

That said, there are many organic constraints on factional power. Our democratic structures are built to accommodate effective action by an intense, effective faction—but not succumb to it. If you use the Internet correctly, it will allow your group to exert its influence with maximum power. This is a good thing. And you can also expect to be constrained by the interplay of other dynamic forces both on and off the Net. This also is a good thing.

But still, what could a group accomplish with 3 million active community members? 100,000 members? Even 10,000? A lot? Yes indeed—a group of this magnitude that will mobilize on an issue is very influential in the policy debate. A player rather than a spectator.

Other groups are beginning to catch on. Brave prediction: MoveOn will not have the field so much to itself much longer. Witness www.AmericanSolutions.com, based in Palo Alto with David Kralik as its Directory of Internet Strategy. Just recently, www.AmericanSolutions.com moved almost 1.5 million people to provide their email addresses with its "Drill Here. Drill Now. Pay Less." campaign. Will it be able to convert these names into a viable, persistent, and self-aware community? Will it be able to find issues that will sustain it? Only time will tell. If it follows the dynamics that govern success—such as communicating with its list regularly and compellingly and assisting that list into becoming a community—it will seize the chance to become a really powerful force in the policy debates.

AmericanSolutions.com is merely one recent emergence. Another is http://dontgomovement.com, which set out to bring Congress back to vote for energy issues. According to its resident djinn Eric Odom, this site saw 60,000 visitors on August 4th as a result of a wave of mainstream media and blog attention. Although Odom is savvy about politics, policy, and the Web, this effort—which is based on a time-specific issue—may or may not prove sustainable. It is a significant bellwether nonetheless. And the coolest use of the pound sign the Webster has seen. (Undoubtedly inspired by the use of what the Tweeters on Twitter call the hashtag, which is helpfully described by http://twitter.pbwiki.com: *Hashtags are a community-driven convention for adding additional context and metadata to your tweets.*)

Among center-right groups, Americans for Tax Reform and Americans for Prosperity appear exceptionally well-positioned to emerge as Web leaders. This is due to the inherent populism of their cultures, their willingness to take calculated risks, the astuteness of their leaders, and their demonstrated willingness to lead with passion, wit, and verve.

Left, Right, or Center, the same rules for using the Web powerfully apply to us all.

Content Is King

The Internet does *nothing*. It is a medium with which you can reach many people at very low cost, and engage them in profound ways. That doesn't guarantee that they'll be interested in what you offer—or even know that you exist. And yet, many groups build websites on a *Field of Dreams* model: "If you build it, they will come." This is a nice adaptation of Say's Law ("Supply creates its own demand"), but it also betrays a fundamental misunderstanding.

It is as if they believe that installing a telephone will cause important people, or important numbers of people, to begin phoning and offering to join their group or provide resources. Or they believe that the mere ability to phone someone's office, or many offices, will make their calls welcome and effective.

What you have to say, and how you say it, is key to successful use of the Internet. The Web is an important medium, and yes, as Marshall McLuhan famously said, "the medium is the message." The critical ingredient is the clarity and pertinence of your message in the context of an attitude of egalitarian inclusion—not your webvehicle.

This, of course, echoes Pulitzer's Law. But experience has demonstrated really beyond quibble that it is mission-critical for you also to propound an action item, one that your visitors will find relevant and not merely interesting, in order to get big and powerful.

If what you give voice to is relevant, compelling, and action oriented, it will indeed allow you to bring together and offer some gentle leadership to thousands, even millions. So you must learn to communicate crisply, naturally, and from the heart.

How do you provide excellent content?

First, your team needs an excellent, confident, clear, prolific writer.

Second, encourage user-generated content. Give your community its voice!

Third, there is an abundance of quality material on the Web that you can legally and ethically use for your site. There is material that is out of copyright, in what is called "the public domain." There is fair use of copyrighted content, a subject that requires expertise and is worthy of mastering. Of superb, too often overlooked, value are materials that are made available for use, with quite modest restrictions, under an elegant system called "Creative Commons." Lawrence Lessig, professor of law at Stanford University, created this deceptively simple, profound legal innovation. The Webster believes that Creative Commons is critical to the Web's long-term vibrancy. Creative Commons is enabled by a small nonprofit group that publishes www.creativecommons.org. In its own words: *Creative Commons provides free tools that let authors, scientists, artists, and educators easily mark their creative work with the freedoms they want it to carry. You can use CC to change your copyright terms from "All Rights Reserved" to "Some Rights Reserved."*

This protocol, inspired by Open Source, does for Web content something very like what the Open Source Movement does for Web technology. Learn it and use it. *The Webster has licensed you to reproduce this book, without charge and with minimal restrictions, under a Creative Commons license. If this is useful to you, thank Lessig.*

The Wikipedia also is an invaluable resource for Websters. Although mostly taken for granted, it—like Creative Commons—is another extraordinary cultural breakthrough based on Open Source principles.

It requires a great deal of diligence to keep your message fresh, relevant, and engaging. So use all the tools at hand.

What happens if you don't pay enough attention to content? Imagine, if you will (to quote Rod Serling), that you built a worldwide TV broadcasting news network and didn't hire any producers or journalists. Yes, all you would have to show would be a perpetual Test Pattern....

or... endless reruns...

... and very few people would come back a third time.

Your team must provide content for your community.

Content is king.

It's a Team Effort

The rewards of success on the Web are disproportionately large in comparison to the effort and risk involved. To do all that it takes requires building a dedicated team that works to enrich and promote your Web presence something as close as practical to 24/7, regularly and confidently interacting with your community, living and breathing the mission.

One of the most powerful inhibiting factors in getting going on the Web is how daunting it is to find a really good technical and design team. How do you find someone talented, honorable, and reliable? Where do you even look? (A word of caution: Many clients have been burned by providers who post on craigslist. *Caveat emptor*.)

Even if you find solid, capable developers and designers, these live in a world far removed from the arcane one of politics, policy, and advocacy that you inhabit. (Your world is as mysterious to them—and indeed to most people—as theirs is to you!)

How can you effectively guide them on what it is you need to accomplish and what you need to do to accomplish it? What must your webvehicle look, act, and feel like to be accepted by your organization and by the community you seek to build? How can you have it built so that a layperson can use it with ease? What are your short- and long-term priorities, and what is your strategic objective? These are some of the major issues that need to be capably handled in designing and building the site.

Really think through what your team is going to *do with* the site. What content will it contain? How will you attract visitors and repeat visitors? How will you go about educating, motivating, and mobilizing those visitors? Your clarity about this will enable your technical crew to provide you with options and let you decide what your webvehicle will look like and do.

Of equal or even greater importance: Who belongs on your team and who is capable of powerfully using, not simply managing, your webvehicle? What kind of skills and disposition do they need, and how much authority and autonomy will you give them?

These points may seem not obviously related to your ability to manage a Web developer. They are, however, essential. There will be a division of labor between you and your technical people. You cannot do their job, and they cannot do yours. Once you have reached clarity on how, and to what ends, you wish to manage your Web presence you will be positioned to direct your developer—if you have chosen well—to develop a powerful platform for your team.

Does the Web Lean Left?

There appear to be no structural reasons why comparable groups of other ideological stripes are not yet very much in evidence. Many studies indicate that self-identified conservatives outnumber self-identified liberals by almost two to one. Conservatives certainly have access to funding, and tend to be very favorable towards technological innovation. Conservatives certainly believe in community.

So why is the Right so underrepresented?

Observe:

The brief history of the Web as an advocacy tool provides a clue as to why the Left has held dominance: a historical accident. Pariser and his colleagues, notably the militant Zack Exley, mastered the medium early and quietly offered tutoring to others who shared their progressive views. Trippi again:

Early on, we had gotten some guidance from MoveOn.org, a pioneer in using the Net to raise money and awareness for political causes... MoveOn didn't support the Dean campaign, offering its help to all nine of the Democratic Party contenders. But we were the only ones who accepted the offer. And so Zack Exley from MoveOn came over to show us what had worked for them. (p. 117)

(*National Review*'s Byron York, in his definitive *The Vast Left Wing Conspiracy*, reports that it was Trippi who reached out to Blades and Boyd, who, to appear even-handed, offered MoveOn's help to all of the Democratic candidates. When, as expected, the other campaigns spurned the offer, MoveOn then dispatched Exley to campaign headquarters for two weeks of training the Dean campaign.)

In addition, of course, and as noted to the Webster by political intellectual Jeffrey Bell, the "out" party tends to get on to new technology first. Conservatives mastered direct mail in the early 1960s, well before the Liberals. There is no reason to believe that the Left has any natural power to dominate Webspace. By happenstance they got there first and brought their colleagues along with training, mentoring, and the inevitable progression of people leaving a masterful organization and bringing their earned mastery to other organizations.

MoveOn makes a very worthy adversary for the Right, one from which it is well worth learning. Many conservative groups have attempted to promulgate a conservative MoveOn. In almost every case these efforts faltered. The cognoscenti assess that these self-styled community builders were really top-down efforts to impose an agenda.

There is a technical phrase for doing this. It's called "putting lipstick on a pig." (Written *before* Obama's insensitive use of this cliché. Love you, Sarah!)

To give another example of the ethos of Web management, one outside the advocacy sector but inside the nonprofit sector, consider Jimmy Wales, founder and reigning archangel of the Wikipedia. Wales is the instrumental figure in building the eighth largest site on the Web, serving over 60 million visitors a month, a site that by Internet rule of thumb is worth billions.

The Wikipedia is owned and administered by a nonprofit entity that has been opposed to accepting even minimal advertising and has hundreds, perhaps thousands, of enthusiasts as contributors, stakeholders, and valued community members. It's "open-source" and self-governing in a very classic, New England town meeting kind of way.

2

WHAT SHOULD THIS THING COST?

Imagine, though, the donations flowing in to your group!

Y OU CAN ACQUIRE A PERFECTLY serviceable webvehicle for between nothing and $20,000.

Unless you are a lone ranger like Matt Drudge, who labored away in relative obscurity for years until he had what the young journalist Thomas Cheplick calls his "Monica Moment," it is wildly unrealistic to expect to generate a massive success on a $10,000 or even $20,000 budget. It happens, but rarely. That's a fair budget to get a decent semi-custom dynamic website built. But that's just the beginning.

Success requires a talented and motivated team. And such a team is costly. It, not the building or technical administration, will be your major cost center.

On the other hand, many an ambitious organization has spent millions on the Web with little or nothing to show for it. Having lots of money is not by itself the key to success. Having enough money and following the rules of Web 2.0, that is what is essential. As the Webster has already noted, the most trenchant running critique of most of the failed efforts to emerge with power on the Web is that they were "top down"—trying to impose an agenda rather than build a community. TV is about "top down." The Web is about building a community with opportunity for its members to be heard and to make a difference.

FreedomsWatch.org, a militantly conservative site formed in early 2007, is rumored to have spent $30 million (not by any means all on the Web effort) and is widely considered to have little to show for it. It is self-described as

formed to be the conservative voice fighting for mainstream conservative principles—today, tomorrow, and for generations to come. We engage in grassroots lobbying, education and information campaigns, and issue advocacy to further our goals and objectives. We create coalitions and collaborate with like-minded groups and individuals to further our common goals.

This approach is utterly top-down and predictable, skipping right over the crucial community-building stage directly to attempts to mobilize. To see so much money being wasted is rather sad, although its reported major backer could well afford to squander ten times as much money without noticeably diminishing his stack. Not sad for *him*—just for Freedom, which always can use some watching. Sad, anyway, for the Webster.

Much of its bankroll, of course, was spent on advocacy advertisements and related purposes. A substantial sum went to an impressive office and team including an accomplished senior staff of about 20. By most reports, the failure is thought attributable to the backers not investing the team with sufficient authority and tactical flexibility— including flexibility to embrace the laws of the modern Web.

Another recent high-profile failure was Unity08—an effort to create, in effect, a third political party on the Web. It was reported, shortly before it scaled down to a skeleton, to have over $1 million cash on hand. It was a self-described "audacious" project backed by some extremely smart people who deserve tremendous credit for willingness to experiment with the Internet. It simply failed to ignite.

Pariser: *"We all have stories about setting up Web sites and nobody came."*

Why did Unity08 fail to take off? Possibly just a matter of timing, possibly a matter of bad luck; but most likely it was deficient content. Unity08 was about "process"—and the masses never get excited about process. They—OK, We— get excited about real people and real issues. All Websters: take note! Let's not project our fascination with the Process onto normal people. All normal people wish for is that their values be respected, their interests served, and their dignity honored—in common-sense ways.

However, even if your cause is compelling it may take some trial and error to find the right approach. If your organization is not prepared to take calculated risks—some of which inevitably will fail—it has no business pursuing a Web-based strategy. The Webster gently points out that an effort to go from a standing start to something big is intrinsically entrepreneurial. It's not called a "startup" for nothing, and it is not without risk. Yet...the potential rewards outweigh the risks by orders of magnitude.

NEVER DOUBT
THAT A SMALL GROUP
OF THOUGHTFUL
COMMITTED CITIZENS
CAN CHANGE THE WORLD:
INDEED IT'S THE
ONLY THING THAT EVER HAS.

—MARGARET MEAD

AmericanSolutions.com had no significant traffic for most of its fairly short life until it found "Drill Here. Drill Now. Pay Less." Then it took off. Then the traffic faded. What will happen next? MoveOn experienced initial success and then hit the doldrums as the impeachment issue faded—until it resuscitated itself by promoting a pacifist response to 9/11. Once again, in Jeff Bell's acute analysis, success often comes from a willingness to stake out the counterintuitive "unpopular" (at the beginning) cause as a niche.

So having bags of money is not required. Nor is it any guarantee of success. That said, unless a group is willing to provide six-figure resources for building, staffing, and promoting its Web efforts it probably should contain its expectations.

It is unrealistic to expect to build and manage 100,000 or a million members for $15,000. To create and guide a 100,000-member community—for a $200,000 commitment (including covering the salaries of two dedicated, full-time staff members)—is plausible if you understand each element required for success.

One of the objectives of your site, for example, may be to generate enough revenue from your visitors and members to cover operating expenses, help the site grow, and possibly even generate free cash flow to help fund your other operations. After all, a powerful Web presence is necessary but not sufficient to the success of your mission. Success comes from working both on and off the Web. To finance your operations—and to project money into the System you are determined to influence—by using the Web is a realistic aspiration.

It takes time to build your network and establish credibility with your small-dollar donors. An advocacy group—or even a political committee—can fail from being undercapitalized, just as a startup company can fail. And keep in mind that the big success stories on the Web were engendered in the context of a Big Story that dominated the headlines and TV News for extended periods (the Clinton impeachment, 9-11, and more recently—and to a lesser extent—gasoline prices). Building a million-plus community will depend on catching the Zeitgeist—and getting some mainstream media play in the process.

3

THE STATE OF PLAY AND VISION OF POSSIBILITIES

*Believed piloted by MoveOn's Ilyse Hogue on her way
to a presidential nominating caucus.*

T HE TRUE POLITICAL, POLICY, and advocacy power of the
Web finally is gaining recognition due, in part, to the
overwhelming strategic asset it has proved through deft use
by the Obama campaign and the campaign's wingmen (like
MoveOn). The effort that positioned Obama to beat the
seemingly indomitable Hillary Clinton to the Democratic
presidential nomination was Web-enabled, elegantly

planned, and executed with intentionality by some very smart people.

It has changed the world of politics irrevocably.

The record indicates that Joe Trippi, on behalf of presidential candidate Howard Dean, was the first political strategist fully to grasp the potential of the Web in politics and make full use of it in a high-profile campaign. The McCain 2000 campaign was an interesting precursor. Somewhere in Cyberspace, in justice someone should be erecting virtual statues of Trippi.

Web-based strategy has been used masterfully by some campaigns (by the Obama team, by Joe Trippi on behalf of Howard Dean '04 and by Trevor Lyman, in a surgical way, on behalf of Representative Ron Paul, for example). And clumsily by others.

Unfortunately for Senator Fred Thompson, for instance, his nominally Internet-centric approach turned out to be like relying on spontaneous combustion. And there is an old saying in politics (coined to describe nominating convention floor demonstrations): "spontaneous as arson." The failure of Thompson to ignite online is widely believed to be attributable to the refusal by someone close to the candidate to delegate sufficient authority to his Web team.

According to the Thompson Web strategist Sean Hackbarth in a private interview with the Webster: *Thompson and the campaign leadership had to care enough to engage the online community. When he did (e.g., around Michael*

Moore and pre-Iowa videos) he was effective and generated online energy. He was very inconsistent. But the campaign eventually understood online's value. A real-time fundraising counter was put on the site encouraging supporting Webloggers to organize fundraising 'blogbursts.' Without that fundraising I doubt Thompson could have afforded to compete in Iowa and South Carolina. They really started getting online's importance, but it was too little too late. (The much-loved Sen. Thompson recently announced the creation of FredPAC and launched his Facebook presence with 12,403 supporters. The Webster is staying tuned.)

By contrast, the Obama Web phenomenon—including its tsunami of money and activists—was ignited by design, not by accident, by people who have a powerful grasp of the state-of-the-art Web dynamic. It was moved by the determination of some very smart cookies—most of them initially outside the Obama campaign structure and very much outside of Washington, D.C.

Although the Obama momentum was a "netroots" phenomenon, those online activists could not have reached their potential without the shrewd guidance of a handful of discerning leaders, most of them behind-the-scenes figures whose names are known only to a handful of Web "digerati." How this was done will be examined in greater depth in a later chapter.

The Obama campaign and its Web strategists by no means preempt the field. There are a number of stars and rising stars on the Web, too many to list them all. We all have, and the Webster has placed special emphasis on, the opportunity to learn from the work of the leaders who have seized the opportunity to use the Web to transform the world. Among these are:

- *Joe Trippi*, who, as previously mentioned, pioneered the political use of the Web for the Howard Dean presidential campaign

- *Eli Pariser*, also previously mentioned, the serene Lama of MoveOn.org

- *Patrick Ruffini*, who from 2005 to 2007 served as eCampaign Director at the Republican National Committee

- *Trevor Lyman*, the outside-the-beltway strategist behind the dramatic "Ron Paul Moneybombs" that raised, from small donors, $4+ million for Dr. Paul on Guy Fawkes Day (11/5/07) and $6+ million on Boston Tea Party Day (12/16/07)

- *Cyrus Krohn*, the mystery man who recently left a very senior position at Yahoo! to be eCampaign director for the Republican National Committee

- *Erik Telford* of Americans for Prosperity, currently viewed by some insiders as the leading candidate to become the Eli Pariser of the Right.

Their work, and their lessons, have not been fully assimilated by the Washington culture—whether in the advocacy, policy, or political communities. These pioneers, and a handful of others, clearly understand that the future already is upon us.

Why is the future now rather than someday soon? How has the Web silently changed to make this possible?

Widespread adoption of broadband Internet access (up to 89% in 2008, according to a recent report by Nielsen Online, from around 50% in late 2004 and 10% in 2000) is one big change. Until fairly recently most people were constrained by bandwidth from fully enjoying the capabilities of the Internet. The proliferation of broadband dramatically changes the playing field.

Now hundreds of millions of people can receive rich content, like video, without having to wait through interminable downloads. And they can upload as easily as they can download. Hello YouTube, hello MySpace. How does this matter? In a word, "macaca," as Sen. George Allen found out when using that word, much to his regret, in a small gathering. In a word, "cling," as Barack Obama discovered when he characterized small town voters as "bitter, they cling to guns or religion" at a gathering of loyalists.

Another factor: Due in large measure to the "Open Source" movement among Web techies, there has been a dramatic reduction in costs associated with the making and using of Web properties. Open Source is the David taking on the Goliath of the Internet giants.

The Open Source Movement is one of the great under-appreciated stories of the World Wide Web. In his classic *The Cathedral and the Bazaar* Eric Steve Raymond, a leading exponent of this movement, explains, or tantalizes, thus:

> *[R]elease early and often, delegate everything you can, be open to the point of promiscuity.... No quiet, reverent cathedral-building here—rather, the... community seemed to resemble a great babbling bazaar of differing agendas and approaches...out of which a coherent and stable system could seemingly emerge only by a succession of miracles.* http://www.catb.org/~esr/writings/cathedral-bazaar/cathedral-bazaar/

What this means, in practical terms, is that huge, informal, free collaborations take place on software programs whose code is made public rather than kept secret like the formula for Coca Cola. Open Source has led to many wonderful programs such as the (free) Mozilla Firefox browser—which runs rings around Internet Explorer and Safari and can be downloaded free from www.Mozilla.org. (People still are trying to figure out how to make money from open source, though, which may explain why Microsoft's Internet Explorer, a badly inferior technology, is used by about 70% of people. And now we shall see how Google's Chrome fares. The Webster guesses: beautifully.)

Open Source has led to a massive proliferation of efficient, inexpensive, and potent platforms (proprietary websites, open-source websites, YouTube, MySpace, and MeetUp, blogs, vlogs, podcasting, and collaborative collections of information called "vlogs") that make constructing and managing a Web property surprisingly affordable.

As Patrick Ruffini, wrote, slightly hyperbolically, in his blog on April 18, 2008:

When the right idea to energize the Six Million [members of a political party's base] comes, it won't come from a "MoveOn of the right" occupying a D.C. office suite funded by an initial round of 7-figure commitments. It will come from someone working outside their den in far outside the Beltway hosting a little activist website that hits the right message at the right time on a $7 shared server.

Ruffini, an authentic Internet virtuoso, is making an interesting point here. Only a few institutions have shown themselves capable of using the Web powerfully. That may not be accidental. Institutions, whether on the Left or the Right or the Center, are inherently conservative and deeply risk-averse.

Ruffini almost certainly is exaggerating to make a point about the "little activist" with the $7 shared server. Only a tiny handful of figures even arguably fit that model—Matt Drudge, Marcos Moulitsas Zuniga, Trevor Lyman. And some of the MySpace and Facebook Obama enthusiasts....

Very few of the major Internet success stories were brought about by one guy (or gal) and a shared server. Success almost inevitably is brought about by a team, with sufficient resources, a great idea, discernment, good timing, persistence, and… blind luck. This is true on the commercial side with companies such as AOL. It is true on the advocacy side as well.

Therefore, it is more likely that the emergence of the Web in Washington will come through a few small and midsized political, policy, and advocacy groups who decide to really go for it. Larger groups, such as the AARP and the NRA, tend to cling to the conventional and, in fact, have very little need of venturing out into the unknown.

It is small and midsized groups who are most likely to grasp how deeply the Web cuts the overhead and administrative costs of assembling and mobilizing large numbers of people, and how greatly the Web can leverage the work of a few people to help mobilize millions. And these organizations can do themselves a service by breaking the conventional caps on compensation for these positions. Success on the Web is a big prize. Nonprofits, whether they recognize it or not, are in competition with K Street, Madison Avenue, Silicon Valley, and other highly lucrative places for the best and the brightest. If you underpay your team you will not keep the best. Under-compensating your stars is penny wise and pound foolish.

Thus, although $100,000–$250,000 (or even more) is a lot of money for even a midsize organization, if it succeeds in assembling a million devoted members—or even 10,000 devoted members—it can prove a wonderful investment. Properly cultivated, these community members readily may donate, on average, $20 a year each in contributions. 50,000 members each contributing even $5 a year would recoup a

$250,000 annual budget (for staffing), by far the greatest cost of maintaining a first-class site.

Moreover, there is a natural law out there somewhere that dictates that only one or two groups can dominate a sector. Groups that are ambitious to seize the leadership in their area will find themselves motivated to take what is called in the tech sector "first mover advantage." That means getting serious about the Web NOW, not someday, when another group, perhaps a friendly rival group, will already occupy what could have been your space.

The Webster wrote this book primarily for those who lead small and midsized policy and advocacy organizations. The Dictionary is directed at those passionate enough to take some moderate, calculated risks in order to make a real difference.

And yet, here's hoping that out there this work will find one reader who just might take inspiration from the increasing simplicity of launching on the Web. Take the "how to" provided herein and meld it with your own passion and smarts to become, in Ruffini's words, someone "hosting a little activist website that hits the right message at the right time on a $7 shared server."

Democracy, fundamentally, is all about embodying the will of the people, with their common sense and common decency. It is surprisingly good at that, especially when the people engage and provide clear direction to their officials. The emergence of the Web fits with this perfectly.

The Web cannot readily be bent to the purposes of despots, although despots and authoritarians have succeeded, perhaps only temporarily, in its suppression or subversion. (Hello Prime Minister Putin! Greetings, President Hu! Funny meeting you guys here. Not that the Webster's calling you despots or anything. Just ...come join us on the bright side of the Force. If Darth Vader could do it....)

As it turns out, the Web is invested with the same principles as democracy. And as the Web's inventor Tim Berners-Lee pointed out, "the Web will always be a little bit broken...." Just like democracy.

The popular will is classically expressed by elections. Elections will always remain the fundamental force, as they must. Elections are occasional—typically held only every 2, 4, or 6 years. Yet, elected officials—the best ones, anyway—are exquisitely attuned to discerning the wishes of their voters throughout their terms in office. If they are not good at pleasing voters, they won't last long as elected officials. Elected officials typically are rather good at working within the framework of their constituents' wishes, duly balanced with the wishes of various elites such as the media, contributors, pressure groups, all of whom, in all their intensity, must be taken into account.

The Web, by allowing people's voices to be heard more clearly, enhances democracy. It has only begun to show glimmerings of its potential. Our descendants shall pity, and marvel at, us. Yet even those early glimmers show how the Web is by its nature biased towards the popular will. Which means biased towards Good.

Our elected officials typically are excellent at straining out the signal from the noise that comes from their constituents. Arguably, it is one of those things at which a good politician must be talented. Let's make it as easy on them as possible by mastering the new media and using the Web effectively and ethically to move America—and, by its example, the world—into an ever more successful, citizen-driven future.

For the "kid with the $7 shared server"

This is a shoutout to encourage Ruffini's activist with the $7 shared server.... Just a few sites dominate most of the Web traffic. So this has a bit of the old Mickey Rooney/Judy Garland "Hey Kids, Let's Put on a Show" to it.

It's a great dream, and very occasionally, as with Matt Drudge, it actually happens. Once in a while, one person, with almost no budget but with a strong grasp of how to use the Web's elements to propel their effort, can assemble a community that rockets to success.

The key principle of success—at whatever scale—has recently come to be called the Law of Viral Loops, which the Webster has attributed, semi-arbitrarily, to Gina Bianchini, CEO of Ning.com, as Bianchini's Law. Ning provides simple, easy-to-set-up, inexpensive private social network frameworks that enable you to create your own Myspace for your own community. The Webster predicts that this will soon become a staple component for many advocacy organizations.

Although she did not coin the term Viral Loops, she, in collaboration with the unceasingly brilliant Marc Andreessen, has brought it to the fore in a most extraordinary way.

In her August 12, 2008 Ning.com blog entry about the design principles for a Ning social network (or any other site). Bianchini is extraordinarily perceptive:

Ah...simplicity. To me, simplicity means showing up on a page where there is a clear focus and purpose.

One of the things we occasionally hear from people is the concern that social networks on Ning are a bit overwhelming with a ton of stuff going on. It's a fair point, but one that is not inherent to Your Own Social Network for Anything.

Our strong belief is that people should have the freedom to create the exact right social network for them. They should be able to add what they'd like and have as much freedom as possible. That being said, I'd like to make the strong case for simplicity in social networks.

http://blog.ning.com/2008/08/the-case-for-simplicity.html#more-3409

Want to use the Web to transform the world? Go ahead.

4

OVERVIEW OF RESOURCES

If you are on a PC, this is what's in your minitower.
Get a Mac already!

T HIS IS AN OVERVIEW OF THE various kinds of Web-based resources available to an advocate or policymaker. A great number of factors will prove common to any site. Yet the sort of influence you wish your Web presence to have will have a lot of relevance to your site's design and structure. In other words, until you decide where you are trying to go with the Web it is impossible to decide how to get there, or what assets should be marshaled to bring you there.

This chapter provides an introduction to the building blocks for a Web 2.0 site. Web 2.0 means a modern, dynamic website that takes advantage of the natural forces of today's Internet.

The basics of a fine site include:

- A good domain name. Preferably something short and memorable. Short is better than long—fewer keystrokes—but memorable is invaluable. No hyphens. Something in which you can own the dot com (as well as, if appropriate, the dot org; you probably need not bother with the rest of the extensions). Don't worry about having a great domain name. With very few exceptions (such as insurance.com) a domain name is more like a vanity license plate than a prestige address. (More details on domain name selection in Chapter 7.)

http://www.thewebstersdictionary.com

- A clean homepage that takes the readers directly into the action—no need to click around to find out what's offered.

- A field on the homepage's upper-facing right-hand corner for the visitor to voluntarily type in his or her email address (and, preferably, name) in return for receiving your Breaking News Bulletins (NOT your newsletter—newsletters are boring). Make it clear that they can unsubscribe with a click. And resist the temptation to ask for more information here; you can do that inside. You are collecting basic contact information—don't make it feel like a census form.

- A good, bold graphic and space for a big lead item and a limited number of subsidiary items. Don't clutter. You are enrolling people, not educating them, on your homepage.

- A donations button (or buttons). There are many options, depending in part on the volume of donations and whether that volume calls for hand-processing or automated handling.

- Room for an RSS feed. RSS stands for "Real Simple Syndication," and all you need to know is that you will tell Google or Yahoo to read about 4,000 publications for you every day, cull the articles that are most relevant to your community, and post a brief description and link to them here. Free. And that you can use it to send your content out to subscribers as well.

- Highly recommended for most sites: a GeoVisitors map. This is a map of the world that will automatically stick pins into itself showing where your last 500 or 1,000 visitors came from, geographically. It gives visual dynamism to your site by showing just how popular it is without creating work for your team.

- A navigation bar at the top of the site to invite people to go deeper within to find articles and videos; an internal search engine to find something filed in the site; a links page or column to let people go to other sites of value to the community, and a store where they can buy, courtesy of www.cafepress.com, t-shirts, coffee mugs, and other merchandise featuring your logo or slogan.

- Links, on the bottom bar, to your terms of service and privacy policy. California law requires that you post a privacy policy; to insulate yourself somewhat in common law, you'll wish to post a terms of use. (For more on this subject, see Chapter 11.)

- An email link, not too prominent (you don't really want to encourage your site visitors to send emails to you too often, it can be overwhelming), where people can give you feedback if there's a serious problem.

Deeper in the site:

- An articles section for news, features, and analysis.

- If relevant, a directory in which people can register and list themselves to encourage interaction between you, your local leaders and rank-and-file members.

- If relevant, a community builder component so you can have your own private Myspace-like social network.

- If relevant, a videos section, so that you can have your own private YouTube.

- If relevant, a "wiki"—which is a user-generated collaborative encyclopedia on a topic of interest. (Wiki is Hawaiian for "quickly," having nothing to do with wicca. So stand down, Christian Coalition!) But create one only if you have enough engaged visitors to flesh it out.

Behind the scenes:

- Web security measures to minimize the chance of your getting hacked.

- A utility to back up your site content to a disk on a regular basis so that if you do get hacked, you can revert to a backup version, minimizing the loss.

- A statistics module so you can keep track of how many people are coming to view your site, how often they come, where they come from, how many pages they view, and which pages they view. You also will wish to keep track of how many are opening your emails (or not). This is invaluable information that you should reference regularly. Without knowing as much as possible about your visitors, you are flying blind.

- A database (typically an SQL—short for Structured Query Language) that will keep all of your email addresses neatly filed away.

- An email utility, so you can send out emails, at no cost, to your list of subscribers.

- Content and category managers, to permit you easily to upload text and pictures to any element of your site, from the homepage to the articles features—and to patrol and edit the user-generated content so that when someone uploads something vastly inappropriate you can take it down. (You may wish to approve posts before they become public so that you can weed out as much of the vandalism, adult-themed content, and other inappropriate material as possible before it goes out for all the world to see. This tarnishes the spontaneity of the experience, however, and whether to proactively edit visitor posts represents a judgment call that each group will need to make for itself.)

- A donor-management platform that will be able to keep track of who gave you how much money and when—and will keep this information on its own server, safe behind a really strong firewall where it cannot easily be hacked.

Now you know. For those who wish to drill down deeper into the difference between Web 1.0 and Web 2.0, here goes.

THE WEBSTERS' DICTIONARY | 49

Web 2.0 is fashionable slang for a website that takes advantage of the newer capabilities of the Web. Web 2.0: folksonomy, usability, economy, remixability, simplicity, standardization, participation, the long tail.... But for most people it is sufficient to summarize it. Web 2.0 is defined by three major qualities: It is easily searched (see Google); broadband (see YouTube), meaning it supports large data packages such as streaming video; and contains user-generated content (YouTube again, MySpace, and Facebook). Moreover its content is right up front, minimizing the amount of clicking around the users have to do to find what you have to offer.

(From the seriously trendy you'll sometimes hear talk about Web 2.5 or even Web 3.0. The Webster will leave that for the next edition—other than to say that shortly after publication the Webster expects the Google Android cell phone operating system to push the Web from desk, and laptop, to the handheld. The Webster haughtily has dubbed this Web 3.0. That said, the frighteningly brilliant Esther Dyson, the Angel of the Internet, makes a compelling argument for user-managed-metadata as the coming thing: http://www.huffingtonpost.com/esther-dyson/release-09-dont_b_85822.html.

So maybe handhelds are merely Web 2.9. Dyson is seldom, if ever, wrong.

And just to clue you in briefly, if your developer talks about "cloud computing" he is referring to the distribution of data, and of computing power, off the desk and into a distributed worldwide network of computers—among them "googleplexes"—which is very much at the heart of Web 2.0. Just humor him. He's on to something cool.

In essence, though, Web 2.0 is more about "community building" than "information superhighway." It may be one of the few instances in recorded history where we've torn down a superhighway to build a village, even virtually. Yay us!

Few Washington policy, advocacy, or even political sites have yet taken full advantage of these powers or of the opportunity to build and mobilize a community. Soon more will. Maybe… you will be in the vanguard.

It is instructive, for those with patience, to consider how the Web was formed. Because we are part of a historical narrative and we are here because of what has gone before.

In the beginning—as unimaginable as this might seem—there was no World Wide Web. Everything was all on the desktop (and on in-house networks) and Microsoft ruled, as Los Angeles writer Matthew DeBord wittily termed it, Web 0.0.

The first iteration of the World Wide Web—what is now thought of as Web 1.0—was invented by a young British boffin (British slang for a technical expert) named (now Sir) Tim Berners-Lee, who snuck it through the bureaucracy of CERN, the high-energy physics lab in Switzerland (and archly self-styled "coolest place in the universe"), as sort of a researcher's central filing cabinet.

(For those fascinated by the history of science and engineering, see Berners-Lee's *The Weaving of the Web*. It's an amazing story about the triumph of creativity, intentionality, and humanity over bureaucracy.)

Its point was that different computers ("servers") in remote locations could be networked and key words could be "hyperlinked" between these computers so you could go from information stored in one to information stored in another by the simple click of a mouse—as easily as you could access information in your own computer.

Although the Internet as we generally know it had been in existence since the'70s, few people knew of its existence and even fewer knew how to use it. Email, invented by Ray Tomlinson in 1971, was exchanged mainly between computer engineers and other specialists. The creation of the Internet was greatly helped—strange but true—by the initiative of then-Senator Al Gore too, just as he claimed and for which he was widely and wrongly mocked. Amazed? Two of the Internet's key creators, Vinton Cerf and Bob Kahn, attest to the truth of Gore's claim: http://www.interesting-people.org/archives/interesting-people/200009/msg00052.html.

(Mr. Vice President, in the Webster's scale your contributions here more than outweigh your global warming fretfulness. So...thanks. Now...would you chill out on this climate change alarmism? It's speculating beyond the data and...unseemly of you.)

It took the creation of the first Web browser, Mosaic (and later Netscape) by Marc Andreessen and his colleagues in the early '90s to make it easy for people to look at pictures and text on the Web. By 1995 the World Wide Web was fully formed and became a sweeping public phenomenon.

There were some important limitations to the design of the Web in its early days. First, almost everyone was on "dial-up," which squeezed data through existing telephone lines. The amount of information that you could access was very limited by the narrow "pipes" through which the information had to flow. So it could take quite a while for a picture to download, and streaming video (like YouTube) was way too dense to be practical for the vast majority of users.

Second, the old Web was for most purposes a way for regular people to access, but not efficiently provide, abundant information. Building, hosting, and maintaining a site was so laborious that only a relatively few technically advanced souls could actually manage it and then in fairly primitive ways. The teeming millions would go to the Web to get information (or visit walled gardens like AOL). And although it was called "interactive," the interactivity was largely limited, for the vast majority of people, to very primitive functions like email, chat rooms, bulletin boards, or forums. And yet even this was a huge breakthrough and led visionaries like Steve Case to create then-great companies like America Online.

Things began to change in the early 21st century. The transformation was precipitated by several major technical developments.

First came Google. According to its mission statement, stated with zenlike simplicity (a key to success on the Web):

"Google's mission is to organize the world's information and make it universally accessible and useful." Mission accomplished, or nearly so. Although not the first search engine, Google has had a huge impact in making the Web (and its millions of sites and billions of pages) more accessible and useful.

That said, it would appear that Google's guiding spirits, Larry Page, Sergey Brin, and Eric Schmidt, get it like few have ever gotten it—across the board—and recognize that the opportunity before them is far vaster than their accomplishments to date.

Second, cable, satellite and phone companies began to put broadband into many people's homes. The Web became much speedier, which meant that people could begin to watch streaming video—hence, YouTube and BitTorrent—on the Web.

Third, Web developers invented ways that made it much, much less expensive to develop powerful, versatile websites and web platforms and, perhaps most importantly, let the visitors really participate in a much more sophisticated way than the old forums. Hence blogs, of which there are now over 100 million, and social networks like MySpace.

These are the major architectural factors of what we call Web 2.0: Fast. Simple. Useful. Easy. Open. Inclusive.

A funny thing happened on the way to Web 2.0. Or, actually, didn't happen.

Most of the policy, advocacy, and political websites in Washington remained structured according to the old Web 1.0 protocols. So Web 2.0 came in around, rather than through, Washington. There are a few prominent exceptions, such as MoveOn.org, which under the light touch of Eli Pariser embraced the power of Web 2.0—and never looked back. Some might say that MoveOn—never "based" in Washington—is not a Washington organization. Yet the energy of its community is very much directed *at* Washington. And this, from whatever place or places a site originates, is the wave of the... present.

In an eloquent 2004 interview with *FastCompany*, Pariser summed up his governing ethos, and that of the Web, and of MoveOn, in just a few words:

The whole point is that this [is] not about us, it's about you.... The insider culture will evaporate as people in Washington remember that in the end they're responsible to us. Constant interaction will help revive democracy.... We wanted to close on something that will also work for the 0% Republicans. You've just got to go out there and do it. The potential of this medium is huge, and I hope that out of this thing comes a million things we can't imagine.

A later chapter will go into more detail about the various pieces of a first-class webvehicle. That said, it's easier than you may imagine, with new capabilities emerging with astonishing frequency. Recent developments include things like private social networks such as Ning and KickApps, microblogging such as Twitter, do-it-yourself sitebuilding sites like www.sproutbuilder.com, and widgets to embed in your site like those at widgetbox.com. The Web has become a very rich field. There are too many utilities to use them all, and it would be a mistake—too cluttered—even to try, but…

This is not your father's Internet.

5

SUCCESS STORIES

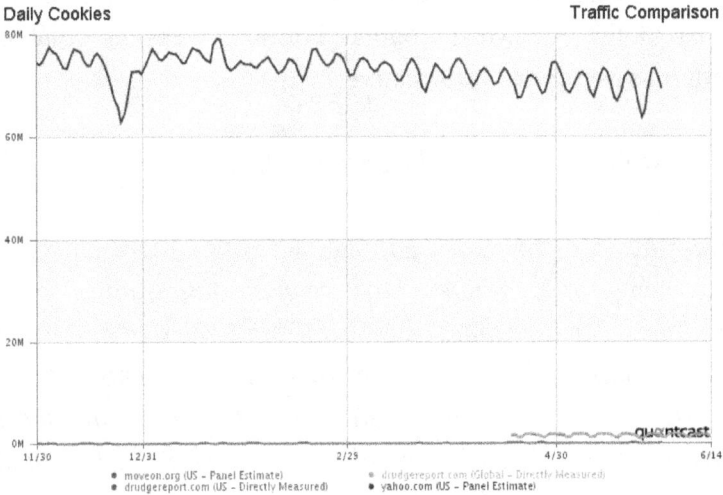

Daily Cookies   **Traffic Comparison**

Source: http://www.quantcast.com/profile/traffic-
compare?domain0=moveon.org&domain1=drudgereport.com&domain2
=yahoo.com&domain3=&domain4=

*You take the red pill - you stay in Wonderland and I show you
how deep the rabbit-hole goes. — Morpheus*

W HAT IS SUCCESS ON THE WEB, anyway? Let's take you
"Behind the Homepage" to appreciate the dynamics of
a webvehicle and take you out of the realm of rhetoric to
understand how many people go there and what opportunities
they may find—or not find—once they get there.

The Webster's purpose is to identify the best practices of the most successful relevant sites and to learn from them how to use the Web to transform the world—not to heap praise on successful sites or even to create a Fodor's Guide to Political Websites.

eBizMBA has already done a better Fodor's Guide than the Webster could. For those who wish to take a tour http://www.ebizmba.com/articles/political-sites recently published a list of the "20 Most Popular Political Websites" that is both interesting and informative:

20 Most Popular Political Websites | April 2008

Over the last few years political websites, representing a wide range of ideologies, have been sprouting up all over the internet many times setting off mini-wars between the editors and audiences of the various sites. This left us wondering which of these sites was becoming the most successful as gauged by overall audience size? To that end, we here at eBizMBA have developed a non-partisan approach to determine the Top 20 Most Popular Political Websites by ranking them by a combination of Inbound Links, Google Page Rank, Alexa Rank, and U.S. traffic data from Compete and Quantcast.

1 | Huffington Post.com
2 | DrudgeReport.com
3 | salon.com
4 | NewsMax.com
5 | Politico.com
6 | FreeRepublic.com

7 | WorldNetDaily.com
8 | DailyKos.com
9 | TownHall.com
10 | NationalReview.com
11 | Christian Science Monitor.com
12 | VillageVoice.com
13 | Alternet.org
14 | TheHill.com
15 | wonkette.com
16 | TheNation.com
17 | RawStory.com
18 | CrooksandLiars.com
19 | InfoWars.com
20 | talkingpointsmemo.com
*21 | littlegreenfootballs.com
*22 | InstaPundit.com

For those who are truly obsessive, there are something like 100 million sites on the Web—nobody knows exactly how many, which is part of the glory of the Web—and there are people (well, software scripts, actually) out there who are busily ranking them all! You can download the list of top *million* sites as compiled by Quantcast.com at http://www.quantcast.com/top-sites-1. *Bon appetit!*

For those who wish to follow the action in real time, Compete.com has an invaluable "Complete Election Coverage 2008" section that tracks campaign site traffic and demographics, as well as blog presence (http://blog.compete.com/election2008/). TechPresident.com runs a discerning watch on all things Web-powered in the presidential election campaign (http://www.techpresident.com/). And TechCrunch is a continuing source of reliable news about what's working on the Web and what's not (http://www.techcrunch.com), sometimes within the Web advocacy sector.

For the purposes of researching and writing this book the Webster focuses rather on sites with particular qualities (and quality). The following 12 Web presences are outstanding successes. They provide, if one looks closely enough, the key intelligence as to how to use the Web to transform the world.

Policy and Political News and Opinion Aggregation:

DrudgeReport.com
RealClearPolitics.com
TownHall.com

Policy and Advocacy:

MoveOn.org
Heritage.org
DailyKos.com
OpenLeft.com
Talkingpointsmemo.com
MichelleMalkin.com/HotAir.com
RedState.com

Presidential Campaigns:

BarackObama.com
JohnMcCain.com

The Webster's list excludes sites that are primarily adjuncts to brick-and-mortar enterprises (NYTimes.com, traffic 12 million; USAToday.com, traffic 11 million; WSJ.com, traffic 5 million). It also excludes sites like andrewsullivan.theatlantic.com that, while modest by way of traffic, have, at least on occasion, enormous impact but are now an adjunct of an established publication. (If Sullivan's site had remained autonomous, www.andrewsullivan.com would have been included in the list. But better for him, a national treasure, to have a steady income than to rely on the tip jar.)

The Webster also excludes sites that, while large, appear to be afterthoughts by powerhouse groups which, for whatever reasons, have not seen fit really to harness the power of the Web, such as AARP.org (Quantcast: traffic 2.8 million) and NRA.org (Quantcast: traffic 159,924). It also, perhaps unfairly, excludes some of the Webster's own favorite sites, such as Cato.org, that have at least until recently presented as somewhat … introspective.

Also disqualified from the list are sites that are fundamentally news or opinion magazines, such as the well-capitalized *Huffington Post*; sites like *Politico.com*, the Webster's personal favorite tabloid (sorry, *New York Post*) which also appears as a print publication in the Capital; the venerable *Slate* and *Salon*; and, for similar reasons, *National Review*, *The Weekly Standard*, and others similarly privileged either with capital, exposure, or an old-fashioned media platform.

With the exception of the presidential campaign sites, which while not representative are extremely informative, the

Webster excluded groups with extensive resources—money and media exposure—behind their sites. Anybody with a popular mainstream media venue or millions of dollars can drive a lot of traffic.

What's really useful in learning how to succeed with the Web with limited resources is what is called "organic" traffic—sites that develop a lot of visitors, notwithstanding the lack of a mainstream media platform or a huge production and advertising budget. Such resources (money and exposure) are unavailable to most advocacy, policy, or political groups. And yet, some break through and others do not.

Different sites have different purposes and accordingly will approach the Web in different ways. It would be a mistake for a policy group to try to perfectly emulate the tactics of an advocacy group, or vice versa. Each will have a different definition of success. The Webster's assessment does not imply criticism of the design or management of anyone's site. It merely is an opportunity to learn from the experience of others.

The dozen sites on which the Webster focuses have two main things in common: They were developed with initially modest resources and they have real impact. One of the lessons that the Webster draws is that there are three "classes" of citizens: spectators, commentators, and players. Many now are moving from spectator to commentator. These stories are about moving from commentator to player.

Most of the successes happen to be mostly Web 1.0 (broadcast) success stories rather than Web 2.0 (community building and mobilization) success stories. This means that some sites are great for providing information and influencing public awareness—and this should not be underestimated. But these mostly don't scratch the surface of the Web's emerging potential to build, focus and mobilize a community.

What do the successes have to teach?

The iconic example of a "Webster" success, of course, is The Drudge Report. One guy, Matt Drudge, reading everything and presenting the most interesting stories, mostly culled from other publications and some from his own sources, has created a news aggregator site that has made him one of the most powerful and enigmatic media figures since William Randolph Hearst.

The Drudge Report perhaps is the most pristine example of the principle that "Content is king." As a matter of design, the Drudge Report is spare. It presents a brief description of, and link to, the most interesting news stories of each day— sometimes of each hour—and by virtue of doing so brings in millions of readers—and tens of millions of page views.

Another simple, highly successful aggregator site is TownHall.com. Built in large measure by, and then spun off from, Heritage Foundation, it is now owned by Salem Communications, which reportedly acquired it in 2006. TownHall collects the best conservative commentary in one place and promotes it through an opt-in email listserv so that leading columns are sent to its subscribers each day. As a result, it reaches something like a million people a month.

A third successful aggregator is RealClearPolitics, which performs a similar function of rounding up each day's most perceptive political commentary, ranging all the way from the hard Left—like *The Nation*—to the staunchly Right, such as columnist Patrick Buchanan, and non-ideological sources such as articles from *Politico*. It also presents ongoing polling data. By doing one thing extremely well—political news and comment—RealClearPolitics dominates its sector and has achieved wide readership and influence.

Moving on to the advocacy sector, one immediately finds MoveOn.

Wikipedia.org provides a brief summary of the 1998 debut of MoveOn:

At the time of MoveOn's public launch on September 24, it appeared likely that its petition would be dwarfed by the right wing's already-impressive effort to oust Clinton. A reporter who interviewed [Joan] Blades on the day after the launch wrote, "A quick search on Yahoo turns up no sites for 'censure Clinton' but 20 sites for 'impeach Clinton,'" adding that Scott Lauf's impeachclinton.org website had already delivered 60,000 petitions to Congress. Salon.com reported that Arianna Huffington, then a right-wing maven, had collected 13,303 names on her website, resignation.com, which called on Clinton to resign.

Within a week, however, support for MoveOn had spread rapidly and exponentially. Blades calls herself an "accidental activist. ... We put together a one-sentence petition. ... We sent it to under a hundred of our friends and family, and within a week we had a hundred thousand people sign the petition. At that point, we thought it was going to be a flash campaign, that we would help everyone connect with leadership in all the ways we could figure out, and then get back to our regular lives. A half a million people ultimately signed and we somehow never got back to our regular lives." MoveOn also recruited 2,000 volunteers to deliver the petitions in person to members of the House of Representatives in 219 districts across America, and directed 30,000 phone calls to district offices.

MoveOn recruited Eli Pariser, who emerged as an Internet activist "in the immediate aftermath of September 11, when he wanted to protest the president's demand for vengeance." Pariser "created an online petition, 9-11peace.org, which urged 'moderation and restraint.' In what would prove a powerful lesson in online organizing, Pariser emailed the link to 30 friends. They did likewise, and so did their friends."

"A few days later I got a call saying the site was crashing because too many people were logging on," Pariser recalled. Within two weeks, more than half a million people had signed the petition. He and MoveOn co-founder Wes Boyd made contact and soon thereafter the two merged their websites.

This brief history of Pariser and MoveOn shows how potent the Web can make even one person, with limited resources, who captures a community's imagination. A rather similar phenomenon occurred within another fervent antiwar community, the libertarians, in 2007.

On something like the other side of the advocacy spectrum from progressive MoveOn, during the winter of 2007, the political world again was turned upside-down by a little-known music promoter from Miami, Florida. A Republican libertarian who had never been involved in politics, his name is Trevor Lyman. The discerning reader will note that Lyman is not listed as representing one of the successful organizations. He was, in fact, about as close as it gets to Ruffini's activist with the $7 shared server (and has, well, moved on from that to an organization that has not yet emerged in a particularly powerful way, but might: www.BreakTheMatrix.com).

The striking success of the two great (and several "small") "moneybombs" that 37-year-old apolitical Lyman exploded for Republican libertarian, anti-war, Congressman Ron Paul is instructive. Whatever he knew or knew not about politics, campaigns, or Washington, Lyman clearly grasped the zeitgeist.

Again according to Wikipedia.org:

In October 2007, while monitoring Paul's appearances in YouTube videos, Lyman discovered a video from James Sugra of California, who advocated a massive one-day fundraiser from Paul's supporters on November 5, 2007. With no political fundraising experience, Lyman devoted his Internet marketing skills to organizing several such fundraisers, which, like some smaller October fundraisers, came to be called moneybombs.

For the first event which he organized, with a solicitation period of about three weeks, he bought the internet domain

"This November 5th" and launched the site on October 18. Aaron Russo's Restore The Republic organization received word of this one day fundraising effort and quickly mobilized its national membership, at the time numbering 15,872, to support this effort. Within 24 hours of Russo's members being notified, over 1500 people had pledged to donate to the Paul Campaign on November 5th. Overnight the word spread to Ron Paul's grassroots supporters, giving This November 5th the needed push to get off the ground. The date commemorated Guy Fawkes Day, recalling Fawkes's attempt to blow up the British Parliament and its modern retelling in the film and graphic novel V for Vendetta *(in which the character "V" seeks sociopolitical change against a futuristic totalitarian society). The moneybomb raised $4.2 million and was recognized by Politico magazine as a pioneering fundraiser in the wake of the McCain-Feingold campaign finance reforms. Lyman's next chosen fundraising date was December 16, anniversary of the Boston Tea Party (when American colonists protested British tea tax policies), widely regarded as the origin of the American Revolutionary War. However, responding to a Paul campaign email, Lyman also organized an interim event for November 30, which raised half a million on short notice. The Tea Party event raised over $6.0 million, the highest one-day fundraising total in U.S. political history. Later events which Lyman scheduled for Martin Luther King, Jr. Day and the Pauls' wedding anniversary of February 1 also collected over $1 million each.*

Lyman commented, "There's no officialness about it in any sense. It's just a website that said, 'Hey, let's all donate money on this day' .... Once the banners were in place and people could start spreading links, it just propagated virally."

Contacted during the course of writing this book, Lyman, who is very busy setting off new moneybombs for his "Strange bedfellows transpartisan alliance" on behalf of constitutional rights and civil liberties in America had this to say:

Those that control the media control everything. The Internet is replacing the old elitist controlled media with one that is controlled by the common man. Today, anyone with a computer can have an impact.

Of course, Lyman's more recent moneybombs have proved significantly less potent—although by no means insignificant: A moneybomb on August 8, 2008 on behalf of a slate of libertarian candidates raised over $150,000.

In a related sector that mixes opinion and advocacy, five site publishers have achieved outstanding success by virtue of their quality, reach, or influence: DailyKos.com, OpenLeft.com, talkingpointsmemo.com, Michellemalkin.com (and her aggregator HotAir.com), and Redstate.com.

DailyKos is the oldest and most renowned of the opinion/advocacy blog aggregators. The brainchild of Markos Moulitsas Zuniga, DailyKos brings in close to half a million monthly unique visitors (according to Quantcast), half of whom are regular readers, giving it almost 20 million pageviews. It is marked by a vitriolic style—and was characterized by Bill O'Reilly as a "hate site"—but vitriol is characteristic of successful opinion/advocacy bloggers.

Kos's influence is extended by his having begun the process of annually bringing together thousands of liberal bloggers at a gathering originally known as "The Yearly Kos" and now known as "Netroots Nation." Kos's prominence delivers regular old media attention, contributing to the "virtuous cycle" of success breeding exposure breeding more success. In addition, Kos recently published *Taking on the System: Rules for Radical Change in a Digital Era.*

Taking on the System is an important book. Buy it. It's a treasure. It will give populists (as defined by Jeffrey Bell's key work *Populism and Elitism* as optimism about people's ability to manage their own affairs) heart. That said, *Taking on the System* is about … taking on the system. The Websters' Dictionary is about transformation. We perpetuate *paralysis* by trashing, rather than respectfully opposing, our adversaries. The Landmark Forum offers a profound lesson. *There is a fundamental difference between change and transformation.* There is room for principled tactical alliances between the Right and Left, *which would transform the world.* Meanwhile … Kos, knock off the vilification. It's juvenile, cheap, and beneath you. It will turn *The Daily Kos* into the Left's FreeP.

There are many, many other liberal bloggers and blog aggregators with a big reach, such as mediamatters.com, rawstory.com, and crooksandliars.com, among others. The Webster considers some of the best to be MyDD.com, OpenLeft.com, Jane Hamsher at FireDogLake.com, and talkingpointsmemo.com. Together, they and other such blogs make up the heart of what are called the "netroots" of the Democratic Party. The Webster, subjectively, considers OpenLeft and talkingpointsmemo especially superior in their quality of content—perceptive and interesting analysis clearly stated—and, as a result, with a superior quotient of transformational potential.

On the Right, Michelle Malkin taps into the passion of her readers in a way somewhat comparable to Kos, both with her own www.MichelleMalkin.com and her companion aggregator www.HotAir.com, which together reportedly reach almost a million people a month.

Whether all of these sites will prove effective at moving the mainstream political discourse remains to be seen. The nearly legendary FreeRepublic.com (known affectionately as the Freep), with reportedly around 1.6 million monthly uniques, did not make the list of success stories. Why? It comes across as a "walled garden" where like-minded Paleoconservatives go to share information and commiserate. It does not appear organized to project, or capable of projecting, energy into the political culture at large and making itself influential, much less transformational. Therefore, the Webster scores the Freep as a sterile force. Whether Kos or Malkin similarly end up as walled gardens (admittedly large and splendid ones) or project the sort of impact that talkingpointsmemo or RedState show remains to be seen.

The transformative power of www.RedState.com cannot reasonably be disputed. RedState privately reports to the Webster that it enjoys around a million monthly unique visitors, sometimes slightly less, and, at points of heightened public interest, many more. According to knowledgeable and highly regarded sector insider (and Red State contributor) Soren Dayton, among others, RedState is the most heavily read conservative publication among Republican Capitol Hill staffers—and is one of five key daily inputs for the enormously influential Mr. Limbaugh.

One of the things that distinguishes RedState and is propelling it to prominence is that it is a source of news rather than merely opinion (or, as is too often the case on the Web's 100 million+ blogs, opinion about opinion). RedState breaks news. Furthermore, its guiding spirit, Erick Erickson, doesn't suffer fools gladly and sets a nicely no-nonsense, acerbic tone. Proving, once again, that Content is king.

Moving into what almost constitutes a different universe, there are the presidential campaigns. There are those, including the Webster, who view everything in Washington through the lens of presidential politics—the World Series of politics. Presidential campaigns are completely unrepresentative—they have too much money, too much exposure, too much prestige—they command attention in a way that has nothing to do with the average upstart Web presence. And yet, because the Web has proved essential to underdog insurgents—Dean in 04, Obama in 08—who started with very little by way of resources and used the Web to become influential, campaigns have much to teach us.

Let's start with the Obama campaign, looking at some of the underreported aspects of how a relatively few people used the Web to help transform the world—by elevating Obama from a novelty to a nominee.

Obama's own Web presence reportedly was for the most part powered not by Washington insiders but by Silicon

Valley figures, such as Mark Gorenberg (a partner in the San Francisco venture-capital firm of Hummer Winblad) and Facebook co-founder Chris Hughes (who in early 2007 took a full-time leave of absence to assist Obama and create www.MyBarackObama.com). The convergence of the power of MoveOn, a few Silicon Valley virtuosi like Gorenberg and Hughes, and Facebook led to a perfect storm that, combined with David Axelrod's caucus-state strategy, propelled Obama to the Democratic nomination.

The backstory from Silicon Valley has not been told in full detail, and telling it is beyond the scope of *The Websters' Dictionary*. *The Atlantic Monthly's* Joshua Green has provided the best exposure to date with "The Amazing Money Machine"—http://www.theatlantic.com/doc/200806/obama-finance—whose message Valleywag distilled in this 98-word excerpt:

If the typical Gore event was 20 people in a living room writing six-figure checks, and the Kerry event was 2,000 people in a hotel ballroom writing four-figure checks, this year for Obama we have stadium rallies of 20,000 people who pay absolutely nothing, and then go home and contribute a few dollars online. Obama himself shrewdly capitalizes on both the turnout and the connectivity of his stadium crowds by routinely asking them to hold up their cell phones and punch in a five-digit number to text their contact information to the campaign.

Consider, then, Obama's "spontaneous combustion" at Facebook....

Obama clearly has the kind of *Smooth Operator* glamour, GQ style, rhetorical eloquence, and JFK charisma that enchants and excites, especially people of the Starbucks demographic. These are real, valid assets. In the words of astute cultural critic Virginia Postrel, in her extraordinary work *The Substance of Style: how the rise of aesthetic value is remaking commerce, culture, & consciousness*, "Aesthetic pleasure itself has quality and substance. The look and feel of things tap deep human instincts."

Obama was able to draw on his superb "look and feel" (as well as an interesting new, at least rhetorical, approach) to mobilize hundreds of thousands of young people on his behalf. And notwithstanding the help the Obama campaign got from Silicon Valley insiders, what happened on Facebook had more than a little of the "Ruffini Activist" to it.

As of Feb. 5, 2007:

There are more than 100 Facebook groups supporting Obama's candidacy, and the group that spawned Students For Barack Obama now has over 56,000 members. It is not the most populated group supporting Obama, but works closely with the largest, "One Million Strong For Barack."

That group was started by Farouk Olu Aregbe, a 2005 graduate of the University of North Dakota. Aregbe said his group has grown faster than any other in Facebook's three-year history. Over 220,000 members joined between Jan. 16, when the group started, and Feb. 5.

(Source: Feb. 5, 2007 report by CBS's Arnie Seipel)

One Million Strong for Barack, as of June 7, 2008, had 548,631 members.

There is an interesting side story about the creation of a fan site on MySpace by member Joe Anthony, and the awkward way in which it was subsequently taken over by the Obama campaign. This story was thoroughly told by Chaoslillith at Daily Kos in May 2007. Those as interested in such matters as the Webster can learn the details at http://www.dailykos.com/story/2007/5/2/35114/27244.

And MyBarackObama? As Bob Ostertag writes in *The Huffington Post,* http://www.huffingtonpost.com/bob-ostertag/reality-time-at-mybaracko_b_110553.html?page=3: *The Obama campaign, by far the most Internet-savvy presidential campaign thus far, operates several web sites. BarackObama.com is a straightforward campaign site, where visitors can see videos of speeches, read about issues, and or course donate money. MyBarackObama.com is a full-fledged social networking site built along the lines of Facebook. Once a visitor registers as a MyBarackObama member, he or she can post blogs, join discussion groups, send each other messages, organize events, and create networks of "friends," just as on Facebook or MySpace.*

In fact, MyBarackObama.com is actually a Facebook knock-off, shepherded into reality over a year ago by Facebook co-founder Chris Hughes. The Obama campaign's early recruitment of Hughes, which enabled the campaign to pull a virtually bug-free social networking site out of its hat early on in the campaign, was one of the most pivotal yet least noted turning points in the presidential race.

As the Webster is typing this, however, there are signs that the McCain Web strategy might be overtaking Obama's in effectiveness. According to Ruffini in a July 27, 2008 analysis:

The common wisdom is that BarackObama.com is not only better at wrangling donations from the faithful, but is categorically better than JohnMcCain.com because it embraces an interactive as opposed to a broadcast model. Time's Michael Scherer put it this way last April:

"Even today, if you go to McCain's website, you are more likely than not to find a page that just asks for money and broadcasts the campaign's message, with issue papers, press releases, and videos.

"By contrast, Obama's website is engineered for engagement: prompts invite people to volunteer, make phone calls and find nearby events. 'Don't just fill out this volunteer form and wait,' it reads. 'Get started on your own.' The blog is maintained by a former journalist; the social-networking function is managed by a founder of Facebook."

I don't disagree as far as BarackObama.com's depth of content goes. But let's not kid ourselves. At its core, BarackObama.com is not truly interactive. It is transactional.

The first time you hit the Obama website, you'll get a splash page prompting you to sign up for the email list. This is good practice, as the sign up form can get lost in the message-of-the-day clutter of the homepage. This way, you can change the homepage at will while still focusing on the most important thing: getting new people to sign up.

But the difference on BarackObama.com is this: the homepage above the fold hardly ever changes.

The main graphic on BarackObama.com has been the same for the last three weeks: Join Barack at the "Open Convention," leading to a donation form. This is what they've had up ever since they announced Obama would be delivering his acceptance speech from Invesco Field in Denver.

And what about Obama's much-touted Berlin speech? The story about Obama's European trip is the second item in the homepage feature, and video of Obama's speech is three deep.

This is no different than what they did in the primary. The majority of the time — from January through June — the main homepage graphic was a toteboard of all the states leading to a contribution page. This should look awfully familiar to everyone by now.

Conventional wisdom holds that major websites should change daily. But Obama flouts this conventional wisdom by hitting every user 1) once with a signup splash page, and 2) with a constant ask for money as the prime feature on the homepage, even if there are more current or important stories to tell.

This is neither good nor bad, but suggestive of the fact that the Obama homepage is compulsively metrics-driven. The campaign would not use this graphic if it did not produce more money than the alternative — even if the alternative was newer and made more sense intuitively.

As the frontrunners online, the best of the Democratic campaigns tend to be more boring and less innovative than their Republican counterparts. The transactional imperatives evident in the Obama homepage and email program suggest a well-honed machine run like IBM at its peak, not a hungry, innovative startup. We know that splash pages and static asks for money work. So why change?

The Web is also becoming more savvily used by political campaigns, by advocacy groups, by news outlets, by think tanks, by PR and lobbying groups ... even by individuals.

http://www.engagedc.com/2008/07/28/baracks-boring-website/

Even some of the savvy Lefties are beginning to pose questions about Obama's vaunted Web work. Kos himself, quoted (according to Jacob Freeze at MyDD.com) in a *New York Times* story, made this observation: "The Obama campaign is still very much a top-bottom operation. They've made it very easy for people to hop on the bandwagon, but those in the back of that wagon still get no say in where the campaign is going." This almost overlooked critique was publicized by Ostertag at CommonDreams.org (http://www.commondreams.org/archive/2008/07/03/10079/) and brought to wide circulation by *The Huffington Post*, July 2, 2008. Ostertag's take:

Well, this week it started to get really noisy in the back of the wagon. A new "group" started on MyBarackObama.com called "Senator Obama—Please, No Telecom Immunity and Get FISA Right." By last night there were 7,000 members. At noon today there were 11435, just short of making it the largest group on the MyBarackObama site. During the time I wrote this column, more than 800 more signed up. By the time you read this, it will almost certainly be the largest. There is even a contest being organized to see who can predict how many members the group will have by the time of the FISA vote next week.

Note to the Obama campaign: even a cursory glance at the history of social networking on the Internet MySpace, Facebook, YouTube, and Twitter for starters) shows that when content creation is put into the hands of the users who also have the ability to communicate and share with one another, the result becomes highly dynamic and unpredictable.

So here we are, balanced at the precise point where the bottom-up dynamics of Web 2.0 meet the top-down dynamics of an American presidential campaign. (Emphasis added.) *Depending on your take on Obama, you might imagine the Senator as railing in private against the power his Internet advisors have unwittingly given his base, or alternatively, as being secretly delighted at the unruly democratic spirit his campaign and its Web tools have unleashed.*

Accounting for How Washington Really Works in Designing Your Campaign

Many forms of Government have been tried, and will be tried in this world of sin and woe. No one pretends that democracy is perfect or all-wise. Indeed, it has been said that democracy is the worst form of Government except all those other forms that have been tried from time to time.

> – Winston Churchill, speech, House of Commons, November 11, 1947. *Winston S. Churchill: His Complete Speeches, 1897 - 1963*, ed. Robert Rhodes James, vol. 7, p. 7566 (1974)

Elected officials, and thus candidates for elected office, care most intently about being elected, or re-elected, or elected to higher office. This entails being thought well of by the majority (everyone would be preferable, but they are realistic) of the people who are likely to vote on election day.

This is so simple, and so fundamental to democracy, that it is often overlooked. It is the Axis-of-Good on which our political system is based.

In order to gain and keep a good reputation among their potential voters, elected officials—the successful ones anyway—care preeminently about five things:

- What their voters (also known as constituents) wish from them.

- What activist groups (who have credibility with those constituents), such as corporations or labor unions, wish from them.

- What campaign contributors (none of whom are permitted to donate potentially corrupting sums of money, although "bundlers"—those who raise money from many—are highly esteemed) wish, so that they can raise enough funds to buy campaign advertisements to present their record to the voters at election time.

- What the party leadership, which controls committee assignments and other assets and resources—including access to nomination for higher office and help in races—wishes.

- What the media (especially local media, such as network affiliates' local evening news) is saying to the voters.

(There is a sixth factor that rarely, but impressively, presents itself: Matters of passionate principle—such as John McCain's willingness to risk forfeiting his party's presidential nomination if that was the cost of advocating what he viewed, it turned out correctly, as the honorable course of conduct in bringing a victorious end to the war in Iraq.)

So, for a community to be influential on officials (and on the elite opinion stream, which is influential on officials), it must be relevant to one or more of these factors. It has to touch the appropriate official's voters; touch, move, and inspire an activist group; become a source of campaign contributions; influence party leadership; or affect (or, in some cases, become) the media.

There is an obscure story about FDR, as reported by William J. vanden Heuvel, in an address entitled *Franklin Delano Roosevelt, A Man of the Century*. It contains one of the most perceptive observations about the political process ever made and is key to understanding how to bring about transformation.

FDR was, of course, a consummate political leader. In one situation, a group came to him urging specific actions in support of a cause in which they deeply believed. He replied:

"I agree with you, I want to do it, now make me do it." (Emphasis added. http://www.feri.org/common/news/details. cfm?QID=954&clientid=11005)

Many Washington websites, and perhaps the majority, are devoted to persuasion, rather than pressure. It is as if many analysts or advocates are more interested in winning arguments than in winning.

Elected officials, typically, happen to be very bright people. They are especially bright in people smarts and street smarts (or they do not remain officials for long). When an idea is presented to them, assuming that it does not contravene a core principle, they will do a quick, and usually accurate, mental accounting of how voters, activist groups, contributors, party leadership, and the media will react to it.

It rarely takes an intricate logical discourse for them to grasp the essence of the proposal. Sometimes a fuller-scale briefing—or internal analysis—is helpful in a complex case. Ordinarily, however, the official immediately will grasp the implications—both to his or her prospect of re-election as well as the welfare of the Republic.

Nor do most ordinary rank-and-file citizens—voters—require, or desire, elaborate persuasion. Even the most thoughtful voters rarely desire more than is included in the op-ed page of the leading daily newspapers such as the *Wall Street Journal* or the *New York Times*, or thoughtful magazines like the *Atlantic Monthly, National Review, The New Yorker, The American Spectator,* or *The Weekly Standard.*

Typical voters, who are also very smart, will decide whether "cap-and-trade," for instance, is a policy they would support based on quite sound instincts as to how dangerous climate change might actually be (versus how much it is being hyped by ideologues or those who stand to benefit from federal appropriations or regulations), how effective the proposed remedy is, and how expensive it will be. Is it really worth $8/gallon gas, if that's what cap-and-trade really means, to reduce CO_2 emissions?

Voters are smart. And it's up to them, ultimately, to decide. Them is Us.

And yet, most Washington websites (not to mention an ever-growing surfeit of blogs) are heavily freighted with position papers, analysis, opinion, and argument. If earnestness were gold, most Washington Websites would be Fort Knox. But it's not and they're not. There are a small handful who could be considered "Fort Knoxes" of policy. Heritage. Cato. Brookings. And they do so by the quality of their content. (Which, repeat after the Webster, is king.) As for too many others, in their joylessness there often is a faint resemblance to Moscow under Brezhnev.

If earnestness were gold we all probably would be talking Russian by now. Much of what is offered on the Web is sterile in terms of shifting the public discourse and outcomes. Most ordinary people are at best marginally interested in reading position papers, online or off. This is a matter they happily delegate to pundits, who distill this stuff and report back, or to their advocacy groups, like the National Rifle Association or National Council of La Raza, to whom they look, with justification, to provide a trustworthy succinct assessment.

As a consequence, most Washington websites attract relatively little traffic. And among the traffic that they do attract, they have modest demonstrable influence outside their own communities—often, surprisingly little influence within their own communities.

The Web is not a magical other dimension. It is a new medium, with distinct properties. One of these properties is that it puts real power into the hands of the visitor to the site. For one thing, visitors are only one click away from departing for more interesting places.

Thus, acting on the Web in a way that either respects or ignores human nature brings about the same results as it does in the "real" world, but amplified hundreds, thousands, or millions of times over. Simply stated, if you bore people, they will leave quickly and likely not come back.

If you engage people where their hearts are, about what matters to them, many will become enthusiastic members of the community you are building, seek the guidance (not education) you will provide for them, and, as they themselves are moved, mobilize with you.

What Is Doing It Right?

How should one define a Web presence as successful?

There are many ways. But the Webster proposes five as fundamental:

- The number of people coming, and coming back, to the site.

- How engaged they are with the site. Are they passersby? Or community members?

- How often do they visit, how many pages do they visit? Are they building your community by enrolling their friends?

- Enrollment of your visitors in taking a stand for the Cause (such as by donating money to you or through you as a conduit).

- Real-world results.

Every serious Webster should fully use the capability to measure:

- The number of "unique" visitors each month (the number of different people who have visited the site at least once during the month).

- The number of visits (some unique visitors come more than once) .

- The geographical source of the visitor (obviously, if you have a site about repealing the death tax in America visitors from Romania or Mongolia are of marginal interest at best—and yes, your site will know and report to you from where your visits are coming).

- The "bounce rate," or how many pages of the site a visitor views before leaving.

- How well your site mobilizes its visitors (for example, by donating to your organization or directing money through your site to a candidate or a cause).

- Whether your visitors are willing to give you their email address. (This enables you to reach out to them rather than exclusively relying on them to come to you. Email addresses are the crown jewel of webvehicle assets.) Do they respond to your emails? How?

At a minimum, you need to fully assess such matters to make even a rough evaluation of a website—and of your level of success. If you care to, you can learn even more details about your site, such as site demographics—the age, gender, and education of your visitors—and where else your visitors tend to go. The latter can reveal some odd facts. For example, Quantcast reports that visitors to Cato.org tend to follow both the paleolibertarian Lew Rockwell and the suave, ultraliberal Barack Obama. (Common denominator? Both are anti-war.)

In the light of the scope of what a few groups have achieved on the Web, some find it disorienting to realize that even the sector giants… are tiny compared to the leading destination websites. In the graph at the beginning of this chapter, downloaded from Quantcast in June 2008, shows Yahoo! (in red) vs. DrudgeReport (in green) vs. MoveOn homepage (in blue).

You have to look really, really closely to see the mighty MoveOn's homepage traffic…almost contiguous with the X (bottom) axis. This is humbling for any aspiring Webster, but also should give you a sense of how little of the Web's potential for policy impact has been explored and how much the future holds for web advocacy.

The implication? This is the dawning of the Age of the Internet. Even the success stories, with their ability to mobilize money, citizens, and voters, are merely providing a taste of what is to come—what is coming now—what you and your organization can accomplish.

Or, to reprise Pariser's Dictum:

The potential of this medium is huge, and I hope that out of this thing comes a million things we can't imagine.

The Universe is just being born. The fun is just beginning.

6

LESSONS LEARNED

Where it's @.

WHAT DO THE WEB'S successful policy/advocacy/political sites have in common?

The Webster propounds Ten Laws to succeed on the Internet.

They are summarized in this book's final chapter. Here's a sneak peek at the list:

1. **Pulitzer's Axiom**
2. **Nast's Law and Boss Tweed's Complaint**
3. **Clarke's Second Law**
4. **Beecher's Law**
5. **Lazarus's Law**
6. **Metcalfe's Law**
7. **Bianchini's Law of Viral Loops**
8. **Trippi's Law**
9. **Pariser's Law**
10. **Cage's Law**

For now, let's see what we can learn by looking at an average, mediocre website.

After that, let's compare it with MoveOn—even if tiny by Web standards, far and away the most intelligently designed, well-managed, and effective policy or advocacy and political/pressure site on the Web. And the most successful.

Average, meaning mediocre, sites primarily present facts and arguments.

Mediocre sites typically do not, or don't often, present the burning-up-the-wires-today events. It's almost as if there is a fear of immediate relevance. Or fear of passion.

This means that they are...academic...in tone. That may be all they wish to be. If so, they are so entitled, but this limits their potential reach for the most part to those involved in the joys of argument rather than practical concerns. The "chattering classes" are an important part of the political ecology but play a much smaller role in policy formation than most of them believe.

However, without diluting your standards—without engaging in sensationalism—you *can* make your site much more dynamic. You can supplement, or even shift, your content and presentation in a way that attracts and energizes many readers.

People won't check in on a website daily unless there's new content daily. And many, probably most, Washington websites update their content only occasionally. This is not attractive—literally. If you keep it current, you will give people a reason to come back regularly rather than rarely.

Average sites provide a "newsletter" feel rather than a "newspaper" feel. Static rather than dynamic. Informational rather than electric.

This is a major lost opportunity to gain and hold people's interest in your cause, to build them into a community, and to enable them to make a gesture that individually would be trivial, even futile, but as part of a concerted effort becomes powerful.

One individual demonstrating on the Mall is looked on as a crackpot. 50,000 are interesting. One million are compelling.

To see what a compelling, dynamic website looks like, check out MoveOn's homepage.

Everything on MoveOn's homepage is current, visual, vital and immediate. There is a personality to every story. And yet—it is rumored that the guiding spirits of MoveOn are dissatisfied with its quality and will be upgrading its site design.

That's the spirit. No resting on laurels.

Everything at MoveOn is vivid, specific, and action-oriented, rather than education-oriented. That's electrifying. To reprise the topics on its homepage from a June view:

Be a part of history. Obama locked up the nomination. Now he needs our help to win. *Contribute to Obama for President. Get your free bumper sticker.* **McClellan: Give profits to Vets.** *Sign the call.* **Oppose the vicious Swift Boat attacks.** *Donate now.* **Help the Victims in Burma.** *Donate now.* **Our contest for best Obama ad had 5+ million votes and has a winner.** *Come see.* **Propaganda revealed.** *Sign the letter.* **Success Stories.** *Watch the Video. See the Climate Town Hall. Buy the Book. Visit the Archives.*

Giving its members some simple (with a click) things to do gives MoveOn.org dynamism. *That built them a list of 3 million potential donors and activists.* They are all about cultivating and mobilizing their visitors. They appeal to people's passion to make a difference. Being dynamic— helping people take action about something they care passionately about—is a small change, technically. Helping people take action is electrifying—a big change, in performance.

Most policy sites are not designed to excite and mobilize. They are designed to inform and persuade. This tends to be recursive, since very few people are likely to come to the site to be persuaded or even to seek ammo with which to persuade others. Nearly every one of an advocacy site's visitors (except for the spies and lurkers from the Other Side, who are opposed anyway) agrees with its point of view before visiting. Laying out arguments repeatedly isn't very likely to swing votes or effect policy outcomes. It's preaching to the choir. Inviting—or inciting!—visitors to DO SOMETHING (even with a simple click) shows respect for their intelligence and for their dignity as citizens. That's exciting to visitors, driving more traffic, mobilizing more resources.

This implies a cultural shift to seeing your visitors not as readers but as community members. It implies abandoning the pleasure of winning arguments to embrace the pleasure of empowering thousands or even millions of people to take action.

Design Lessons

On the design side, most policy homepages would benefit from being pruned back to a much simpler design.

Most home pages are too cluttered and present too many options. People are busy. Few wish to plow through "everything"—especially chained to a flat-panel display screen. Visitors seek and desire your gentle implicit guidance as to priorities.

An information-heavy homepage is like putting the index in the front of a book. Homepage simplicity is obviously part of the success formula for most, perhaps all, of leading sites like MoveOn, TownHall, Drudge, and RealClearPolitics.

Like MoveOn, learn to use the homepage to focus and motivate visitors, not bewilder them. (You can educate, inform, and even, yes, bewilder them on the inside pages if that is your wish.)

Visitors appreciate focus. Indeed, they demand it.

Indexes to a vast amount of information and discourse belong in back or, at most, as a sidebar. There's room for them there. Moreover, your site can have its own internal search engine so people can look for specific information by typing in a few words á la Google, but within your site itself.

Another key: Avoid a repetitive masthead graphic that imparts no new information or special visual appeal. Go heavy on new, ever-changing images—and don't hesitate to ask your visitors to upload pictures to a Flickr.com account, send you a link and then use that.

Add a thumbnail or larger graphic to almost every item. Pictures are powerful. Lore has it that Boss Tweed, the infamous political boss of 19th Century New York City, was brought down by (Republican) political cartoonist Thomas Nast, and that Tweed once demanded of his henchmen:

"Stop them damn pictures. I don't care so much what the papers write about me. My constituents can't read. But, damn it, they can see pictures."

(Tweed was fatally undermined by Nast's cartoons. Lore also has it that Tweed was apprehended, as a fugitive, by Spanish authorities who recognized him from Nast's cartoons. Imagery is powerful. Use it.)

Another way to keep your site fresh and compelling is to install a homepage RSS (Real Simple Syndication) feed that draws on a Google or Yahoo free service which automatically "reads" thousands of newspapers and magazines and pulls out what you designate, letting you present fresh news every day. This is a freebie that provides continual fresh site content of general relevance to your community—with little if any staff effort or administrative work. It's a draw to bring visitors back regularly.

Another simple way of improving the dynamic feel of your homepage is to embed a geomap (a free or low-cost Google Earth mashup). This provides a map of the world and sticks flags into a world map automatically from where the most recent 500—or 1000, or whatever you like—visitors are coming from. It gives readers a sense that people are thronging to you (if they are), engaging what persuasion professionals call "social proof." It also adds visual dynamism with no administrative effort.

Next, use the Web for what it's really good at (and got good at around 2006). Use it to build a community, a community that feels—because it has—a real ownership in the site.

Wikipedia.org has hundreds or thousands of devoted members who have made the patrolling and continuous enhancement of this site, the dominant online encyclopedia, a passionate avocation. The founding father of Wikipedia, Jimmy Wales, acts as a thoughtful, caring hometown mayor-figure facilitating and carrying out community consensus rather than as a dictator (although he is duly teased by community members as such).

An advocacy homepage should feature what's in the news (especially what's controversial, meaning what is most interesting) and give a simple action item after each report—if only to keep the community motivated and trained to be mobilized when you call them to the barricades....

The Web is now approaching the dominant status of TV. In 2004, Joe Trippi showed Howard Dean intimations of the Web's power. (It's not quite clear that Governor Dean exactly liked what he saw. If he had, he might be president now.) Seize the strategic advantage.

7

SITE FRAMEWORK

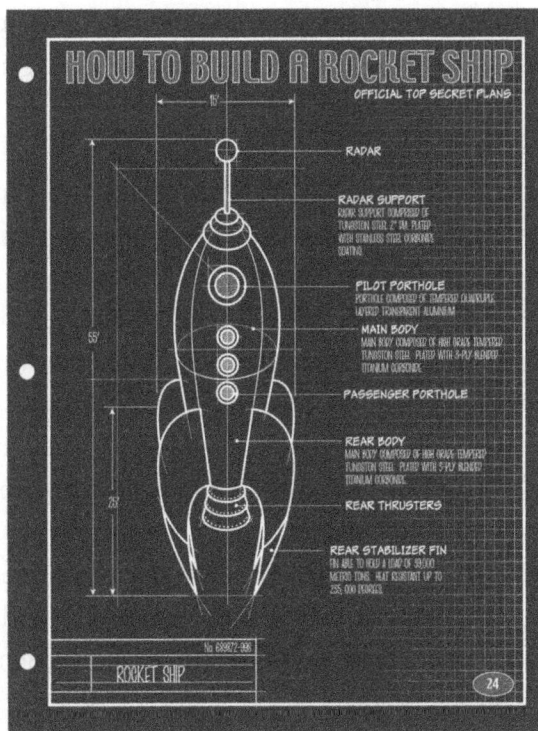

The Secret Blueprints of MoveOn.org? Revealed here? Sacre Bleu!

NOW THAT THE WEBSTER has reviewed the dynamics of Web, and of democracy itself, it's time to look more closely at the nuts and bolts.

Let's take a moment to address in greater detail the most elementary point, your domain name. You acquire a domain name by going to a registrar. That sounds very officious, but really it means that you go to a website such as Network Solutions (www.netsol.com)—which is the senior registrar, and the most expensive but not necessarily best—where you type in the domain name you think you would like. If it's available, you follow a simple procedure to acquire it—either for a year at a time or for longer periods. (They will also try to sell you many and diverse other services, like Web hosting. Let your developer handle this. Stick with acquiring the domain name.)

You can acquire as many domain names as you can afford. Shockingly, some otherwise reputable intermediaries will charge you as much as $1,000 to acquire a domain name for you. Don't fall for it. Netsol will charge $35 per year with discounts for multiyear purchases (slightly higher for certain exotic extensions like .tv). GoDaddy.com charges more like $10 per year for each domain name. There are other registrars who charge even less. Once you are registered with a particular registrar it is a hassle to move a domain name, although it is doable. The Webster recommends that you pick a solid one—GoDaddy is good—and use it exclusively rather than keeping track of accounts with several registrars.

Even if the domain name you fancy is taken, you still may be able to acquire it. Some registrars will let you make an offer on a domain name that is forwarded to the name's owner. Or you can contact the owner directly by looking up the domain name on Netsol and clicking on WHOIS, which will tell you who owns it unless the owner has chosen to make that information private.

However, it's rarely worth paying a premium for a particular domain name. Unless you have something really generic and iconic, whether classy domain names are equivalent to high-end real estate or more like vanity license plates is a matter of dispute. When people are looking for your issue, people who have never heard of your group, will they type in your domain name? No, the Webster thought not. So don't get too wound up in the search for an ideal domain name. Just find one that is good enough.

Here are some good rules of thumb in choosing your domain name:

- Even if you are a nonprofit, only buy a domain name if you can get both the .com and .org. Why? So many people are so habituated to just typing .com that if you only own YourSite.org and someone else owns YourSite.com, your promotion could end up driving people to someone else's website. You can have multiple domain names all feeding into the same website, so even if your website is "SomethingOrOther.org" you can have "SomethingOr Other.com" take visitors there. It's hard enough to get people to want to visit your site; you don't want to lose anyone to domain name confusion.

- All other things being equal, shorter is better than longer. The fewer keystrokes, the better.

- Memorable is better than gibberish. You want people to remember the name of your website from hearing about you on TV or just having read about you in a news story, and nobody can remember alphabet soup. Similarly, watch out for homonyms. And if you use a numeral in your domain name, like Vets4Victory.com, make sure you also acquire VetsForVictory.com to avoid bleedout of visitors to someone else who has taken a similar name.

- It can be useful to have key search terms in your domain name as it can help your page ranks with the search engines. It's a plus if your domain name reflects the purpose of your site but balance this with keeping it short and memorable.

- Capitalization is irrelevant in a domain name. Whether the user types in BigDeal.com, BIGDEAL.com, or bigdeal.com, they'll still go to the same place.

- Preferably do not use hyphens in your Web address. (You cannot use apostrophes and ampersands, the Web doesn't permit it. Yes, you can use numbers or a combination of letters and numbers.) Hyphens are considered slightly déclassé and also you have to say "dash" between each element when you are telling someone your domain name. That's tedious. Avoid hyphens.

- If you already have a Web address with hyphens that has an established presence, just live with it.

- Don't bother with the .infos, .mobis, .bizes, and the other extensions, not even .nets. .net was originally invented for ISPs and, while (unlike .edu or .gov) you can have .net for the asking, you are rather unlikely to need it. If you control the .com and .org, you are basically covered. .tv is kind of cool—the rights to the extension were rented from the tiny island nation of Tuvalu in Polynesia. If you are doing primarily a video broadcasting site, you might want it. Or if you are planning on moving to Tuvalu... The Webster acquired Credibility.tv just in case he ever decides to open a Web-based TV News network.

- Make sure the Autorenew feature is turned on when you acquire the name and keep your credit card information and email address up to date with the registrar so you don't inadvertently lose your domain name. In fact, it might be smart to sign up for the 99-year plan (at a deep discount) if you are serious about establishing a presence on the Web and you have the funds. That way there's no oops factor.

- Netsol—unless you elect otherwise—makes your contact information public when you acquire a website. If you want to keep your information private, make sure you specify that.

- You are legally precluded from "squatting" on a domain name that is someone else's registered trademark. And you can be liable for heavy damages for doing so. It is highly unlikely that this will happen—but if you are worried about it, go to the US Patent and Trademark Office's TESS function to see if someone owns a trademark on the domain name you are about to acquire and if you're not sure, ask your lawyer. If you cannot afford to engage a lawyer on this, go to http://tess2.uspto.gov/ bin/gate.exe?f= tess&state=dc9617.1.1 and check carefully.

Now, on to more challenging aspects of developing a Web presence.

Basic Site Functionality and Platforms

A website can be much more than a virtual piece of paper tacked to the virtual bulletin board also known as the World Wide Web.

There is an avalanche of books—go into any Barnes and Noble or Borders—about the structure and composition of websites, most of them severely technical. We would advise you to read them, but... they are borderline incomprehensible to a layperson. These are written for artisans of the craft, not managers or advocacy leaders.

Rather, this chapter provides most of what an advocacy or policy person needs to know about basic options for the look, functionality, features, and architecture of websites. This should be enough to help you make decisions, and to decipher what a designer or developer is saying if he lapses into jargon. Which he almost certainly will. Jargon is their native tongue.

If you are operating on zero budget, you may wish to post a blog (short for Weblog). There are already over 100 million blogs out there, most of them with very tiny readerships, but a few have large or influential followings. They are free and easy to establish and publicize. If that's what you want, just go to www.blogger.com or www.typepad.com, and you'll be on your way. Most great sites will have a blog as a component. You'll set it up so that your fans can subscribe and receive it in their email. If you are going to blog, the Webster begs you: Only blog if you have something you, at least, find genuinely interesting to say. If you are blogging because you think it is required, or because you wish to show people how clever you are, it is a waste of your time and of the world's precious, scarce pixels. There already are abundant blogs. So have the decency to have a good reason for creating yet another one.

Beyond blogs, there is the intermediate step of setting up a simple Web 1.0 website to be hosted by a company like GoDaddy.com. You can do this at the same time you buy your domain name. Using templates that your host will supply you can create your site framework, upload your content, pictures, and text, and be up on the Web in a day with a very pretty site. Your friends are unlikely to discover that you have done it that way.

That kind of site mostly is like a poster on a bulletin board and may be precisely what you need if you are just trying to Issue a Manifesto, put out a profile of your group, or check off the box on your to-do list that says "get website." If your needs are simple enough you might even go with a service like VistaPrint that will allow you to put up a pretty darn good Web 1.0 site...for $14.97 a month...do-it-yourself...in minutes.

It gets your information out there…to anyone who knows to look for it among the estimated 63 billion or so Web pages out there. (Source of this latest guess as to how many Web pages are out there: Wikipedia June 19, 2008, (http://64.233.169.104/search?q=cache:oNVo9sH5FsUJ:en. wikipedia.org/wiki/World_Wide_Web+how+many+web+pa ges+are+there+2008&hl=en&ct=clnk&cd=11&gl=us.)

Lingering in the "Land of the Free" for another moment, some inexpensive, high-quality options for designing your own Web 2.0 site are currently emerging. For example, you can create your own dedicated social networking site (like having a private Myspace or Facebook) simply by going to Ning.com or KickApps.com. Both of these offer simple, high-performance "off-the-shelf" site platforms that you then can customize with your own content and graphics and further customize with "widgets"—site mini-features (such as the geomaps and RSS feeds described above).

Both Ning and KickApps offer free sites that come with certain limitations (such as, for example, including the name of the host, like "Ning," in your site name and letting them include, and keep the money from, Google ads on your site). They also have inexpensive premium versions that will run under your own unique domain name and will permit you— with suitable buildout effort on the part of a skillful designer (not developer)—to offer many wonderful added features to your community.

However, if you are ready to treat the Web as a serious, mission-critical resource, you will wish to have a grownup website. (You can wrap a private social network inside it.)

For those who want dynamic sites, sites that really perform, but don't have a quarter-million dollars to spend on Web design and development, a semi-custom site probably is the best bet. (Even if you have a six-figure development budget, a semi-custom site probably still is your best bet. Apply the savings to enhancing your team.)

The three leading semi-custom general use platforms are Joomla!, Wordpress, and Drupal. There are also special purpose semi-custom platforms such as Kintera's Sphere. By a semi-custom platform, the Webster means a standardized platform that can be customized both by the use of templates and modules. For example the Joomla! template provider Rockettheme.com can make your site look great. Your developer can integrate modules such as RSS Feeds, community builder sites, email utilities, and so forth.

One of these systems will allow you to have just about all the important features available on your site and at moderate cost (under $10,000, depending—possibly much less). Among the three semi-custom general use platforms the Webster is partial to Joomla! However, Joomla! has the drawback of letting everyone to whom you give administrative privileges have the run of the site, rather than letting certain people have access to only certain elements of the site. And there is a concern that if your traffic gets too heavy—millions of visitors, you should have such a problem—Joomla! might not be able to handle it. (This is called a scalability problem.) On the other hand, Joomla has a better visual look than the boxy Drupal.

Joomla!, Drupal, or Wordpress—or a specialty platform—will give you a versatile homepage with the ability to change text and graphic content about as easily as composing a Word document. If you are not sure which one to use, use this simple litmus test. If you are willing to grant unlimited administrative access to the site to all members of your Web team, go with Joomla! If you need to compartmentalize access, go with Drupal. If you outgrow Joomla! at some point you can, and will be able to afford to, migrate to another platform. And you well might greatly benefit from having specialized features only available from companies that specialize in the nonprofit and advocacy sector, like Kintera, so check this option out carefully.

Modules

Once you have the platform as a foundation, your developer will attach the various modules that make your site interactive in interesting ways. For example, he will install a database that will hold the email addresses of all of your members so that you can communicate with them on a regular (preferably at least once a week) basis.

This will link to an email-sending module, like Letterman, that will allow you send 1,000, 10,000, 100,000, or even a million emails rather quickly and at no or low marginal cost.

Email your members. Why is it important to send email to people who sign up with you? It is an easy way for them to keep up with what you are doing—without their having to remember to go to your site to see if anything interesting is happening.

So—once you are invited to communicate regularly with your community, following through with regular, interesting messages makes the bonds of community much stronger. That said, it is very important to have someone with a knack for writing consistently interesting things succinctly— preferably with an embedded picture, which gives the communication a higher perceived value—in charge of writing these.

Weekly, or twice-weekly, bulletins seem to be in the sweet spot for most people. Less can feel sparse, more can feel intrusive, but it depends on the quality of the content and the engagement of the community. People should be able cancel their subscription ("opt out") with a click; being stickily intrusive is a good way to get a bad reputation.

What should the content be? Keep it informal in tone and write about things the people around headquarters—and, more importantly, the people of your community—are finding interesting. Write about your take on things in the news, for example. Think human interest and feature articles. Were you in the news? Send word around! And never neglect Pulitzer's Law.

The single most important text in an email is its subject line. You may have scintillating content, but if your subject line is bland and uninformative many recipients will not bother to open the email. You should consider your subject line as an important opportunity to communicate. Use it.

There is a utility called a Web Beacon or Clear GIF that will allow you to actually tell whether or not someone to whom you have sent an email opened it. True Websters will take advantage of this capability. If you have 300,000 people on your email address list, but typically only 100,000 open their emails, then your list may be only 100,000 in reality (although a different 100,000 may be opening any given email).

You should be able to do this in-house, but if your Webmaster can't find an email module that incorporates Web Beacons, contracting it out may be the way to go. There are commercial services that will deliver your email and tell you who opened it at a very, very low cost. It might be just the thing for your organization.

Your ever-changing homepage content plus your weekly (or more frequent) emails may be the most compelling content of your site. But wait, there's more! (No Ginzu knives, though.)

Merchandise. Your site—and organization—may benefit from offering site-branded merchandise. There are two fundamental ways of doing this, and both can be used to good effect. The simplest is to wrap in a CafePress.com site that will allow you to sell T-shirts, coffee mugs, and other merchandise that has your organization's logo or message— or anything you care to design—on them.

This helps to build your community and "brand identity." CafePress takes care of all the printing, order-taking, payments, shipping, and returns. That said, CafePress also charges a high wholesale price (over which you build your markup) so this merchandise tends to be expensive. (You can buy it in bulk from them at a significant discount to sell at your conferences, seminars, and so forth. That requires inventory management and handling, a hidden but a real cost.)

Custom Merchandise. It may prove more lucrative—but also entail much more handling—for you to design and sell certain goods via your own merchant account. High-quality custom designed T-shirts might cost $10 wholesale at CafePress and $2 wholesale (not including design costs) if you do it yourself. The Webster relishes the design work of graphic artist Shane "Boredom Is Always Counter-Revolutionary" Becker. So if you need a design you might check up on him at http://theresistancearmy.com and find out if he's willing to do some design work for your cause.

Among things you can sell, eBooks are one of the best. eBooks can be downloaded from your site at no cost or handling to your organization. Real books that you place at a Print on Demand printing house can be drop-shipped by the printer directly to the buyer, also with no handling.

A Print on Demand house like lightningsource.com will charge you something like $4 to print and bind each copy as a quality trade paperback and will ship it directly to the buyer (but whose one-off shipping price is so high you will prefer to do it yourself or outsource it), remitting the difference between your posted retail price and the wholesale price to you. That said, it's a technically finicky process to deliver a camera-ready manuscript to a Print on Demand house, so be prepared to spend some time.

If you have access to some good writers, this can be a great way of helping get your message across, building community, and raising additional funds for your cause. Unless you happen to be running the leading "Free Britney" group, however, your revenues are likely to be modest.

Podcasting. Another module that is showing some potency is podcasting, offered by such organizations as www.LibSyn.com. This allows you to open up your own virtual radio station. Subscribers to your podcast need only click on a link in an email from you and they can listen to your show at their computer or download it to their iPod or MP3 player to listen while at the gym or during the daily commute. For various reasons, podcasting has been much more successful in an audio format than as video, so far.

Video. If you wish to present videos on your site—strongly recommended for many groups—the preferred method is to place the video content on YouTube and then embed a very simple (one-line) code on your site that will bring the video to your viewers without incurring higher hosting charges for the large amount of data that video requires.

Social Networks. The Webster already has recommended the inclusion of a social networking component. To give your community members the ability to present themselves and their thoughts, to develop and maintain groups, to contact one another, and to allow you to interact with them—listening to their concerns—is a major step forward in the community-building power of the Web. And, once again, community building precedes mobilization.

Wiki. If your issues warrant it, you can even include a "wiki"—or user-generated encyclopedia—about an issue important to your community. Be warned, however, that there is a risk that your wiki will attract too few enthusiasts and will feel sparse. Sparse is bad—it makes your site feel like a ghost town. Any component that does not gain traction probably should be depublished—which your site administrator can do with one click.

Directory. Separate from, but related to, a social networking component is a directory. A directory will allow your widely dispersed members to self-identify geographically and find others close to them—only, of course, those who wish to be found—in order, for example, to help build local chapters. Because the Web is most powerful when it integrates life both on and off the Web, the Webster strongly recommends that you learn the simple steps of using MeetUp.com to help assemble real-world communities as well as virtual ones.

Communicating with Officials. For community mobilization to contact officials, a company in Washington called CapWiz has a proprietary technology that you can license and install that will allow your community to locate and send emails to their elected officials such as congressmen, senators, even the president. One of CapWiz's divisions even handles state legislators.

(Emails to the president of the United States are of no significance—they're not equipped to read them over there. The impact of emails to Congress is a matter of some controversy. Emails have far less impact than phone calls and letters from constituents. So: Teach your community to call their Congressman, who loves to hear from the folks back home. That said, generating thousands of "Hill contacts" from constituents can be, the Webster believes, a decided plus in advancing your cause. The CapWiz utility is unquestionably a fast, simple, and expensive way to facilitate this. Other platforms, such as Kintera and Convio, offer their own systems to do this.)

Donations. A key site component—one as important for your viability as the quality of your homepage and smart use of your email list—is a way for people to contribute to you very quickly and easily using their credit card or PayPal. If the number of donors is modest, it probably is most efficient to have your organization's own administration process the donations and keep track of the donors. But as you scale up to many donors it may well become more efficient to automate the process.

There are a number of respected donor management software providers, but active enthusiasm for any system has been difficult for the Webster to find. It is unclear whether this is due to the technology being cumbersome and expensive or due to lack of focus by smaller and mid-sized groups in learning how to use the system efficiently.

Still, if you build a community of 100,000+ people you may find yourself with an embarrassment of riches. At this point a donor management utility will be invaluable and probably indispensable. And you will have the resources to investigate the packages offered by various vendors. (It will be a nice problem to have!)

Take the associated training for the use of these systems seriously. A system is only as good as your proficiency in using it.

Security. Another aspect that will require increasingly strict attention on your part as your site grows in size and importance is security. Security issues—beyond those determined by common sense, like keeping the donor information on your server well protected, and keeping your user-generated content patrolled to remove vandalism—are beyond the scope of this book. These will be handled as a matter of course by a capable site developer but it is good practice to monitor the protocols being observed.

Once you are big enough to attract malicious hackers you should have the resources to bring in specialists if needed. Specialists are expensive, but your exposures are many. If you are going with a dedicated provider like Kintera many defenses will be built in. If you are having your own system built, for instance through Joomla!, be acutely aware of the potential vulnerabilities and grill your developer thoroughly on what he is doing to protect you.

The specialist's Specialist in security is a guy named Bruce Schneier. It is unlikely that you can afford him. Subscribe to his newsletter, www.Schneier.com, so you, like the Webster, can lie awake at nights worrying about everything that can go wrong. As Schneier wrote in 1998: *The doomsday scenario is real: An ethical hacker discovers a security flaw, someone else writes a program that demonstrates it, someone else with less ethics modifies it, and someone with no ethics decides to use it in a way no one ever envisioned.*

Suddenly there's a web site that has a Java application: 'Click here to bring down the Internet.' It's not a pretty thought. (http://www.schneier.com/essay-003.html) Ten years later, the Net's still up. But that doesn't mean it won't all come crashing down tomorrow. Aren't you glad you asked?

Page Ranking by the Search Engines. There is a whole art called Search Engine Optimization (SEO). This is a way of positioning your site to appear higher in the Google (and other search engine) ranks—i.e. to be higher on the page a user sees when conducting a search. It is extremely challenging to game the system to move your site to be one of the top three entries—or even on the first page of search engine results.

The search engines are very sophisticated in determining which are the most popular sites. Google claims that its system takes into account something like 500 million variables in assigning a page rank. These variables include things like how long you have been on the Web, how extensive your traffic is, how many content-relevant sites link non-reciprocally to yours, and other factors.

Once you have abundant resources, you can call in an SEO specialist and see if you can improve your standing, but if you can't get onto page one on the search engine results, for the most obvious searches, the Webster believes it is rarely worth doing. Just be the best you can be, promote your presence intelligently, and the right people will find you.

Advertising. You can drive thousands of visitors to your site by advertising, such as by purchasing Google Adwords.

Note, however, that Adwords are pay-per-click or impression. You are paying for people to just come and look at you. This can be very expensive. You can cap how much you spend, so it's not dangerous, but it's still expensive. Does it make sense to bring in what may be mostly the idly curious? It depends on how many give you their email addresses and become active in the community, of course. If enough people sign up and enthusiastically contribute to you, it can more than offset the cost of the advertising. But it is essential that you do a pilot and a rigorous cost/benefit analysis. This is all the more true, and tricky, for advocacy organizations that are not in search of product buyers who provide instant feedback.

Do you have enough free cash flow to swing a big advertising budget, and a sophisticated analysis of the results to see if you are just bringing in a lot of passers-by instead of community members who will participate and donate? If not, the Webster believes it probably a better use of funds to stick with site promotion—even paid PR campaigns, preferably along the lines of guerilla marketing—rather than paid advertising.

Site Analytics. Finally, you will have access to an extensive instrument panel that provides extremely valuable information about your visitors, how many they are, how often they return, where in your site they go, generally where they came from, and many other significant details that will help you understand what actions you are taking are effective and what actions are futile.

Use your stats module to generate reports and study them. Daily.

8

HIRING A WEB DEVELOPER AND DESIGNER

Web developer and designer submitting a proposal to you, the prospect.

ONE OF THE FIRST THINGS someone who wants a website will discover is that you have to answer a lot of questions. Creating a website is much more of a collaboration than it is a delegation, even if you have plenty of money to spend.

You are looking for someone called, in the industry, a developer. The story really only begins there. The developer fundamentally is a builder, and has, thank Heaven, the psyche of an engineer. He needs to be part of a team, led by you. And your team must include a site designer. (There are a few great designer/developers out there. Count your blessings if you find one.)

Your developer and your designer will possess a very different sort of sensibility and skill set than does your graphic designer—the person who will produce the layout and create, or preferably find, the images that define the look and feel of your site. Both site design and graphic design tend to be almost alien to the kind of person who actually is going to "develop" a website (meaning write the software or assemble the software modules).

There is not one skill set that is needed for successful Web design, development and implementation.

There are six.

The six separate areas involved with creating and using a powerful website are:

- **Site design.** What goes where on a website, both visually and functionally. A great design makes your site much more powerful.

- **Graphic design.** What your site looks like, and the images that are displayed, will determine whether it is strong and appealing or boring, confusing, and off-putting.

- **Site development.** This is the "code" that invisibly makes up your site. Designers do not write code or assemble modules; developers do.

- **Content management.** "Content is king." Great content, clearly written and organized and easily accessed and understood, makes your site powerful. This is your and your team's responsibility, not your developer's, not your designer's.

- **Site promotion.** What if you build a website and nobody comes? You have to go after your audience. Knowing how many people ("unique users") come to your site and how much of your site they come to view ("page views") is essential to knowing whether your site is reaching the people you desire to enroll.

- **Community building and mobilization.** These factors, like content, will be your and your team's job. It's your job to get people to participate in your transformative work, such as by recruiting friends to join your site, by holding a party at their house on behalf of your cause (and letting you know), or by sending money to your organization or its beneficiaries.

So… there are six separate skill sets involved in making and managing a powerful website. How do you get started?

First, you can save yourself much time and grief by not going down what looks like a logical path but turns out to be a very wrong one. To us civilians IT (Information Technology) and Web guys look and sound a lot alike. And you already have an

IT guy who helps to fix your computers when they misbehave, set up networks, deal with file compatibility issues, install new software and additional RAM, and so forth. This is someone who is largely incomprehensible to you when he tries to explain things—but gets the job done. You are grateful to him for handling the incomprehensible and quietly even more grateful when he refrains from explaining what he is doing.

Well, IT guys and Web guys may sound alike to you but the resemblance is superficial. Resist the temptation to turn to your IT guy for guidance. The fact is, most IT guys *think* that they understand the Web, probably have their own websites, and do, in fact, understand some of the basics like how to buy a domain name, set up a simple Web 1.0 site, get it hosted on a server, upload text and graphics, and so forth.

The Web is a specialty and an advanced one. The advanced nature of it has to do with things like being proficient in XML (Extensible Markup Language) versus HTML (Hypertext Markup Language) which many techs know and which is essential, of course, but insufficient to develop for the modern Web.

Don't ask your IT guy either to drive this process or to be critical to your process of finding the right developer. It is a common mistake and almost always a source of massive confusion. Just resist the temptation to lean on your IT guy for this. It won't help you and is unfair to him. He won't tell you this. IT guys are a proud sort. Justifiably so.

Having avoided the mistake of mistaking an IT guy for a Web guy, you still face finding someone to build your site.

You could hire a full-service design shop to do everything for you. This gets the job done but tends to wildly inflate the cost. A website you could create for $5,000 or $10,000, if you know what you are doing, or know someone who knows what they are doing, can end up costing many times that and taking months rather than weeks to build.

So you will most likely need to find both a developer and a designer. As stated above, finding the two in one person is rare; if you can find such a person, recognize that you have struck gold.

In shopping for a Web developer and designer, it helps to understand better the nature of the process, both in the design phase and the operations phase. This will help save you from commissioning something that will prove poorly designed for your purposes or hard to manage.

A website designer will know—really know, in light of what you are trying to accomplish—how to structure your site to make it easily manageable on a day-to-day basis. He will know where to put the content of the site to maximize its impact and let it channel the energy of your constituents, members, stakeholders, community.

You will help him understand what you need to do to get people coming to your site, what they need to find there in order to keep coming back, how to persuade them to lend their energy to your cause, and how that is structured. If you are not confident that he has a feel for this he may not be a good choice for the project.

When the designer's work is done and the developer publishes the site to the Web it will be up to your team to write the copy and select the graphics. It will be up to your team to promote your site to build the traffic.

It will be up to your team to mobilize, at the strategic moment, your community to make thousands of calls to officials. Or perhaps you will use Twitter (a form of microblogging where people can sign up to get "tweets" from you) to form a flashmob (a group that seems to appear spontaneously to protest, or celebrate, something). It will be up to you to help your community figure out which elected officials need to hear, what they need to hear, when they need to hear it, and how to get your community to take action…. And it will be up to your team to listen to the community and take its concerns to heart.

In short, a good website is a microcosm of your world, your organization, and your campaign. There are no shortcuts.

And your team, to be effective, must pay attention to its instrument panel, its "analytics," to learn just how well you really are doing on the Web and to adapt your actions accordingly. Understanding your own role first makes finding the right developer possible.

What to Look For

Ideally, your developer will look exactly like a Norse God, such as M.E. Winge's famous painting of *Thor and the Giants*. (Anticipating developer Knox Bronson doing battle with the Russian site developers?)

Not every great developer looks exactly like this, however. And there are a welter of available functions that a website can possess. Few if any developers are proficient in all of these, although many profess proficiencies that they do not possess. Anybody can call himself a Web expert and many who have a very poor grasp of how to do it hold themselves out as just that. No accreditation bodies certify Web developers and designers. Cosmeticians are subject to stricter licensing requirements! (As to that, cosmeticians are also subject to stricter licensing requirements than members of Congress, Senators, or even presidents. So we have no real grounds to complain.)

To complicate matters, the technology of websites is evolving at lightning speed, so what was cutting-edge last year may be rather obsolete now. Also, as noted (repeatedly) above, most developers express themselves in technical jargon. Frequently, you will have to ask even the best ones to repeat what they just said in something closer to English.

As previously noted, most developers—even those who routinely work in the Web advocacy sector—are unfamiliar with how the policy, advocacy, or political community works. And they may or may not be able to grasp the concept of building a site to build community—especially the nuances of the community you yourself are determined to build.

Obviously, your first recourse will be to seek recommendations from others who have a substantial Web presence. Unfortunately, relatively few advocacy or policy groups have much significant experience in this area. Even fewer report satisfaction.

Your second recourse may be to inventory the sites of organizations that are highly successful on the Web—successful in building a high volume of traffic and a membership that can repeatedly be mobilized in educating and enrolling the public in your cause. And then ask them for advice.

Again, unfortunately, there are a very, very limited number of organizations that can boast of this and those organizations, even if they are willing to advise you, very likely had advantages (a huge initial list á la MoveOn, a multimillion dollar budget á la Huffington Post) that are unavailable to you.

The best ones, like MoveOn, keep their tech in-house. Moreover, if those who contracted the work had a satisfactory experience with a Web development house, the key personnel who engineered their success may have quietly moved on to work elsewhere, perhaps unbeknownst to the people who are providing you with a reference.

Therefore, ultimately you will have to make an independent evaluation of your potential contractors. It helps if you know enough about the underlying architecture of the Web to weed out the more blatant charlatans; this book should help you somewhat in that department.

At some point you're going to have to rely on your— hopefully well-developed—ability to assess people. As you would with a potential employee, try to assess whether they're flaky or dependable. As you would with a car mechanic, try to assess whether they're trustworthy or just want access to your wallet.

Be prepared to embrace a measure of imperfection. As Weinberger says in *Small Pieces Loosely Joined*,

The imperfection of the Web isn't a temporary lapse; it's a design decision. It flows directly from the fact that the Web is unmanaged and uncontrolled so that it can grow rapidly and host innovations of every sort. The designers weighed perfection against growth and creativity, and perfection lost. The Web is broken on purpose. (p. 79)

But embracing imperfection is different from embracing incompetence. Be especially wary of people who over-promise. It is extremely common to find someone who says, "Yes, of course I can do that, for surprisingly little money and very quickly." And then the process mysteriously breaks down. And you are stuck, sometimes indefinitely. Sometimes this is because they're thieves, and sometimes it's because Web developers have a strange tendency toward over-optimism; either way you're left in the lurch.

Get the names of recent clients who can vouch for their ability to deliver on time and on budget. And check these references carefully. This is by no means foolproof but is better than nothing. It is surprising how many clients skip the reference check.

Optimally, you will find a developer/designer who first insists on carefully reviewing your organization's stance, mission, structure, resources, and staff and what you wish to accomplish. If the developer wishes to go through this process, it's a very good sign. Anything less is winging it. For a more comprehensive view of best practices, the Webster invites you to study Appendix B, which lays out a thoroughgoing project management protocol.

A good assessment entails a big investment of time and it is not inappropriate for a developer to ask you to pay for such an assessment. This will allow him to provide you with clear recommendations about what the design and development of your webvehicle might entail. You will own the assessment to use with whomever you choose to retain. And it's a good way to test-drive your candidate to see if they perform a discrete task well, on time, and for a reasonable price.

The Webster believes that the most effective way to facilitate communications with a developer is for him to show you (or for you to show him) comparable sites that are highly effective. This can save a lot of time and misunderstanding.

The best approach that the Webster has employed is to hire the leading candidate to do a modest trial project—a pilot project—outside your main website but relevant to your mission. This gives you a chance to see if your candidate delivers while minimizing the risk to your organization's image and operations.

9

THE USER'S PERSPECTIVE

Note Al Gore operating the crane.

Y OU MAY HAVE NO DESIRE to build and employ a website but appreciate the value of being a more informed site visitor. Websites may look very similar from the outside. They can be as deceptive as the big image of the Wizard of Oz manipulated by the little man behind the curtain. As the old joke goes, "If you read it on the Internet, it has to be true." So it's useful to know how to make a better assessment of the scope, depth, and reach of a site.

One extremely interesting thing to have some idea about is how many people a site actually reaches. One can and should expect different things from a site with a million readers than one with a hundred readers.

So it is recommended that you check out one of the public site rating services, such as Quantcast.com or Alexa.com, which will give you a great deal of information about how many people visit a site. Neither of these sites is definitive—only the site proprietor knows for sure and estimates by outsiders can be wildly off the mark—but both are respected and are so for good reason. That said, their data can be off by an order of magnitude.

There are plenty of "urban legends"—and outright hoaxes—floating around on the Web. Fortunately, the Web provides its own antidote to these if you just know where to look. There are several very reliable sites devoted to anti-disinformation. Snopes.com is highly recommended to find out whether a particular Web story is based in reality. Check it out before you go emailing some particularly outrageous story to your network of friends.

Although the Internet is by nature endless—to quote Carl Sagan out of context, "billions and billions"—as a practical matter there are about 5,000 websites that really matter at any given moment. According to a posting at Microsoft-watch.com, http://www.microsoft-watch.org/cgi-bin/ranking.htm:

Web traffic and linking follow a power law distribution curve. In simple terms, this means that something like the top 10 percent of all websites get 90 percent of all web traffic and all external links. The bottom 90 percent of all sites share the 10 percent of Web traffic and external links that remain. If you have a sense of what people mean when they say that "the rich get richer," then you know what it's like to be a poor Webmaster who is told by his boss to increase traffic to a site.

According to http://blog.jbyers.com/category/alexa/:

The top 4 or so sites on the web do orders of magnitude more traffic than the next 40, who do orders of magnitude more traffic than the next 400, and so on. By just about any measure, Digg and flickr are enormously successful sites - but you wouldn't know it if you took a quick look at a graph of them compared to MySpace. So next time you look at Alexa, remember, it's all relative.

Thus, while traffic moves up and down at various sites, the top 500 or so sites dominate the vast majority of the traffic on the Web and the top 5,000 are the ones that count. This does not mean that if your site merely attracts a few hundred thousand visitors a month, it is inconsequential. Remember, "it's all relative."

For those who wish to stay on the cutting edge of developments on the Web, *Wired* magazine is the hippest publication out there. For the even more seriously geekified, *Technology Review*, published under the auspices of MIT, is indispensable. The blog at Alexa.com is unfailingly interesting and informative. And the really serious techie source of cutting-edge information is Slashdot.org ("News for nerds. Stuff that matters."). Slashdot is one of the biggest and most influential sites on the Web yet is completely unknown to most policy types. It is to techies what Drudge Report is to politicos. It has even been turned into a verb, among techies, to get "slashdotted"—meaning to get written up there and get so many visitors as a result that it crashes your servers. In a comparable category are boingboing.net, engadget.com, and gizmodo.com. Highly geekified and not for the faint of heart.

For Web advocacy, TheNextRight.com and Epolitics.com are superb. Luckily for the world one is a Conservative and one a Liberal voice of excellence about the Web advocacy sector.

The Webster has already referenced Ruffini, one of the principals of TheNextRight, several times. And here's what Epolitics.com's Colin Delany has to say about, well, e-politics:

Let's change the world! But how? Robot/kung fu army? Too expensive. Zombies? Too messy. Online politics? A wise choice: the internet gives ANYONE — candidates, advocacy organizations, corporate interests and everyday citizens alike — powerful tools to mold policy, influence elections and shift the direction of public discourse.

The Webster agrees with Delany's formulation. Zombies really *are* too messy. The Webster's not naming names—but we've seen some in action recently. (They don't know who they are but We know who they are.)

10

SECRETS OF A MASTER SITE DEVELOPER

Photo by Jody Frost, courtesy of Tangerine-Sky Interactive.
Knox Bronson

K NOX BRONSON IS ONE of those rare gems who is a virtuoso graphic designer, site designer, and site developer. He is also an *avant-garde* novelist and an authentic rock star. (Don't believe the Webster? Go to www.knoxbronson.com. His current CD is like vintage Bowie. Like Bowie? Buy it. And the Webster's vast network of spies reports that next he will be taking on "three chords and the truth" Dylan.)

Q: Knox, what is the biggest mistake that prospective clients make in looking for a Web developer?

A: Not asking for, getting, and checking references.

Q: What's the second biggest mistake?

A: Not knowing what they are really trying to do. Part of the job of a good designer/developer is to help them think that through. But the other thing is expecting that all they need to do is just put up a website and it will just automatically transform their business or organization. Really, unless you manage it, update it, and promote it, it will just sit there.

Q: Can you give me a couple of examples of how to promote a site?

A: One of the most charming stories is www.icanhaz cheezburger.com. About two years ago Eric Nakagawa and Kari Unebasami, of Honolulu, created a site where people could upload photos of cats with cute captions. (Very cute captions!) They quickly got to 12 million uniques a month, server-melting territory, then sold it to a businessman, Ben Huh (really!) for $2 million. Get it right and this could be you.

Don't forget traditional PR and promotion—they are still important. The key is to integrate online/offline...don't shortchange your website. Now let me give you a bad example.

I did a wonderfully designed site for a church not that long ago. They had nobody in the organization willing to own the site and learn the very simple process of updating and adding content—which is really no more complicated, technically, than word processing. As a result, they never published the site to the Web and it was pure money lost to them and a complete waste of my time as a professional. They even hired other people afterwards to help them launch it and it never launched. It was a complex site that functioned and looked very nice, with things like automatic calendar updates on the splash page—all the activities in the next week and so forth—and they never used it. Such a shame. The two people who had authority to get the site designed had no interest in keeping it current and couldn't find anyone in the church to do so. Don't let this happen to you!

Q: So, Knox, I know you are very picky about whose work you will do. What do you look for in "hiring a client"?

A: You have to take operations on the Web at least as seriously as you do your other critical-path missions. So, I am not interested in someone who doesn't get it and thinks that a website is some kind of trivial thing that gets tacked on to the job description of someone so junior they can't refuse. Properly managed and promoted, a website can create a framework that will permit literally hundreds of thousands of people to create a community around you or your mission. A website is not a static entity, it is an evolving, organic creation. If people have that attitude about it, that's how it will grow. If you look on it like an online brochure, it's not going to bring you any results.

There's so much that can be done now. Ten years ago, that's pretty much all you could do, an online brochure. Even five years ago, before ubiquitous broadband, the constraints were pretty fierce. Now you can build applications—for example, it makes it so easy for your visitors to sign up for your breaking news bulletins. It's moving so fast, people can customize their pages. You can do instant polls, video comments, all sorts of great stuff. In addition to applications, it has functionalities like an RSS (Real Simple Syndication) feed to populate your own site, or you can create Google or Yahoo RSS feeds using keywords relevant to the interests of your community and publish the results automatically on your site, creating a constant flow of fresh content.

People can actually subscribe to your site and every time you publish a new article they will get an email notification about it so they are prompted to come visit you. That's one application of an RSS Feed.

You can have audio and video podcasts now. An example that I worked on is UnderTheTuscanGun.com, a cooking show broadcast on the Web—which goes into iTunes automatically and sends along a portable PDF of the recipe they are cooking. Thanks to the success of that site, they are getting big endorsements and very likely a major network show. Of course, Debi and Gabriele are great fun to watch and the recipes are great ... another example of "Content is king!"

Q: What are the biggest mistakes that people make in hiring Web developers?

A: There are a few. The first is dealing with a gypsy/bandito from Craigslist. Beware of anything that sounds too good to be true, they will take your money and you will almost certainly get nothing. It could even be worse, as they can get control of your domain name and control it. One client of mine hired someone, with excellent references—a big company—who moved their domain registration to some host in New York and a different registrar, and we're having an awful time moving the domain name back under their control.

Here's a horror story that will turn your hair white. I posted on Craigslist, I got a number of calls, one woman called, the job sounded promising, I knew I could provide what she needed within her budget. And then, I got a call from her to say some Russian company would do the whole site in Flash animation within her budget. I've seen unsuspecting people badly compromised by Russian or Indian—and even American—hustlers, companies that move in, lowball a bid, and then take the down payment, don't deliver, add new charges, and it never ends.....

The other mistake is to go with an IT guy—a programming guy who administers networks—who doesn't really understand Web design—who doesn't think like other people and cannot help you design a site that makes sense to normal people. This is a critical thing.

Anybody that you are working with, in the proposal stage, should propose an overview, a site map, key functionalities, and a site development plan, including markers. For a complex site map—sections, categories, how they are going to get there—something four or five layers deep, you should pay at least $1,000 just to do the assessment of what it will take to develop a serious website.

In one case, I had a potential client who had around 20 active sites and 100 different components and hundreds and hundreds of pages, many of which were duplicates, that needed to be integrated...the inventory on that was about four thousand dollars...the client had built London, so to speak, online, and without the inventory, would have built Bombay the second time around, making it still impossible for a visitor to find the information he or she was seeking.

The third mistake is to go with an established firm who will charge you $50,000 and pay one of their people $5,000, which represents the work really entailed. You end up paying a huge overhead for an account executive, an art director, a "strategic alliance" executive...when all you need is a well-designed interactive website with a solid back end.

Ideally, you really only need three people to build a website. The back-end guy, the artist, and the person who talks to the client and the technical people. The back-end guy writes the code, puts in special features, makes sure that it is all stable and does what you want it to do. The artist lays it out, makes it look nice and easy to move around in. And one person to see how it all goes together and make sure it meets the needs of the client.

Q: After the site is published, what's the job of the developer?

A: The Web is bringing forth powerful new functions all the time. One of the things about a website is that you should consider it a work in progress. What's state of the art in 2008 may be shopworn in 2009. You can do more with less and so you should provide in your budget for regular upgrades to your site to keep it as powerful as possible.

Q: Why is it so hard to understand what the heck Web guys are trying to say?

A: Well, because there are so many technical aspects to Web development. There's the back end—how this stuff actually works and making sure that it all works together. Stuff like collecting email addresses and sending out emails to thousands of people. Stuff like what we call "cascading style sheets" (CSS)—which believe it or not may work in one Web browser like Firefox but will be tricky in Microsoft's Internet Explorer (IE), which is a really terrible browser but about 80% of the world uses it. And there is a whole art, for instance, as to how to fit a website on a visitor's screen. The client's needs, the visitor's needs, what the site is supposed to do. How it looks, how it works.

The right person is trying to help the client, as they go along, step by step, as to how to make these various factors work. I've worked for major telecom companies that have had a committee of 40 people arguing over what to "surface" (put on the homepage), big turf battles. In that situation, discretion is the better part of valor.

People should look for a developer who can explain to them, in plain English, what the issues are. If they pooh-pooh you, find someone else. None of what is happening is especially mysterious and there is nothing mystical or magical about it.

People should trust their instincts. In over 15 years of Web development, my experience is that 90% of the time people know their organization and its needs. You have to be able to help them get it communicated to you. The developer should be asking you a lot of questions, and should be able to tell you what needs to be done, and why, and how… you are the client.

The developer is there to serve you and your audience.

11

SOME LEGAL ISSUES

Internet lawyer (specialist)

THERE IS NO SUBSTITUTE for solid legal advice to back up any enterprise, on the Web or off. This chapter just lays out a handful of issues to get your conversation started with your lawyer.

First, although the Web is worldwide, California law requires everyone to have a prominently displayed privacy policy talking about what you have the right to do with the data your site collects.

To turn straight corners with the law and save yourself the possibility of headaches later on, publish a privacy policy. If your lawyer doesn't have one on her processor you can probably write one by looking at the policies of various sites and adapting them.

After having read dozens of privacy policies, one of the world's dreariest documents, the Webster's current favorite for sheer clarity and readability is that of Ning.com. (Not all of it will be applicable to you.) If you want to see an example of pure gobbledygook read the privacy policy for YouTube or Facebook.

So—make sure you have a privacy policy and that a link to it is posted on your homepage.

While not statutorily mandated it is almost universal practice to incorporate a Terms of Use page, also with a link posted on your homepage. That lays out your rules of the road—what conduct will be permitted and what conduct is prohibited.

Terms of Use haven't seen a great deal of legal action. Recently Twitter got into a big kerfuffle when one of its users complained that it wasn't enforcing its terms by not excluding someone she claimed was harassing her through the system. Be thoughtful about the terms you adopt; let them be about something over which you are willing to make a stand. It is just good practice to have—and enforce—sensible site rules. The Webster strongly recommends that you understand your own Terms of Use and don't just take incomprehensible boilerplate offered by counsel.

Feel free to steal and adapt the privacy policy and terms of use of www.TheWebstersDictionary.com. Don't assume that they've been looked over by competent counsel, though. And if you appropriate these, you might wish to omit the little pet cemetery that the Webster hid in there with tributes to various beloved departed cats and a tortoise. Having a pet cemetery in your Terms of Use is not mandated either by California law or by common law. Neither is it prohibited.

The Digital Millennium Copyright Act provides certain immunities to websites. For example, there are safe harbors for what other people (not you) post on your site—copyright or trademark infringement, for example—so long as you take it down promptly if someone registers a complaint by contacting you through a clear channel that you provide for such purposes.

The Webster urges you to adopt and enforce rules of common decency and common sense, including anti-vilification policies. Whoever you are, adopt and enforce anti-defamation polices and anti–intellectual property infringement policies. Give your visitors a clear way to efficiently and promptly bring violations to the attention of a responsible decision-maker in your organization.

The Webster considers controversy a good thing, generally speaking, and vilification a bad thing. It discredits your site in the eyes of many people, limiting your transformational power. Like pornographic content, vilification draws visitors but injures human dignity and your credibility.

In another area of Internet law: There are hefty fines for taking a domain name that is someone else's trademark. This is unlikely to happen, but if it does, it is a matter for you to take up with your lawyer promptly. Give it up.

If you will be raising money on your website, it may be important to make sure you are registered in the 43 or so states that require registration for nonprofit charitable solicitation. It is rare, but you can be fined very heavily for failure to register. There are law firms that specialize in getting you registered and right with the law and can provide you with one-stop shopping services to get you filed for a very reasonable sum. There are separate rules about collecting and remitting sales tax on merchandise sold on your site. Ask your accountant.

As an advocacy group, your undoubtedly are more interested in getting exposure than in making money from your content. To facilitate this it is valuable for you to prominently note that your site content is licensed under Creative Commons. This is a very simple system to allow people to know that they can, with such restrictions as you choose to apply, reproduce your content and publish it themselves. The Webster has emphasized the value of using Creative Commons material as site content on your own webvehicle. There is potentially even greater value to your cause in offering a Creative Commons license to your own site. Let other people spread your words.

Be aware of these basic considerations as you develop an Internet presence. The full scope of legal considerations associated with working on the Internet is beyond the scope of this book. Consult a good lawyer.

THE WORST CASE SCENARIO   162

12

The Web comes at you fast.

*T*HE WEBSTERS' DICTIONARY now has taken you through the core elements of how to use the Web to transform the world. Because the Web changes so fast, interesting news and features will be provided, without charge, to those who register at www.TheWebstersDictionary.com.

But as Herman Hupfeld wrote, and Sam played for Rick: *the fundamental things don't change as time goes by*. The Webster offers the following laws of "How to Use the Web to Transform the World" as fundamentally unchanging. *If she can take it so can I.*

Each of the Laws, admittedly, is stolen from someone much smarter than the Webster. To justify this theft one could quote from Sir Isaac Newton: *If I have seen farther it is by standing on ye shoulders of Giants.* [Letter to Robert Hooke (15 February 1676).]

In truth, though, the immodesty derives from labor leader John L. Lewis's famous dictum: *He that tooteth not his own horn, the same shall not be tooteth.*

The 10 Laws:

1. Pulitzer's Law:

"Put it before them briefly so they will read it, clearly so they will appreciate it, picturesquely so that they will remember it, and above all accurately so they will be guided by its light."

The very best "mission statement" ever for the Web.

And the Webster's corollary: Give them easy, simple, direct ways by which their voices may be heard and by which they can, individually and in concert, take action.

2. Nast's Law (and Boss Tweed's Complaint):

"They can see pictures."

Stop them damn pictures. I don't care so much what the papers write about me. My constituents can't read. But, damn it, they can see pictures.

The Webster says: Use compelling graphics. No one knows how many words a picture is worth these days, but it's certainly more than a thousand.

3. Clarke's Second Law:

"The only way of discovering the limits of the possible is to venture a little way past them into the impossible."

The Webster says: The Web is not for the faint of heart. We can learn from our predecessors, but we can only win by trying new things and finding out what works *now*.

4. Beecher's Law:

"No great advance has ever been made in science, politics, or religion, without controversy."

The Webster says: Embrace the controversial. Controversy (within the bounds of good taste, common sense, and common decency, regrettably often lost on Beecher) is pure gold. It is interesting, draws attention, drives traffic, and excites the community.

5. Lazarus's Law:

"Unleash the imprisoned lightning."

A mighty woman with a torch, whose flame
Is the imprisoned lightning, and her name
Mother of Exiles....

On the Statue of Liberty is engraved a sonnet by Emma Lazarus, *The New Colossus*. It expresses the message of true populism—humanism—exquisitely. Take its message to heart.

The Webster says: The Web can be our means of unleashing "the imprisoned lightning" of millions whose voices have been exiled and to whom the world *needs to listen*.

6. Metcalfe's Law:

"The value of a communication system grows at approximately the square of the number of nodes of the system. A single telephone or a single fax machine has no communication value. Two phones have a little value. A thousand phones have real

value. A hundred thousand has great value. A million or more, extraordinary value." (As stated by D. Calvin Andrus in *A Complex Adaptive Intelligence Community: The Wiki and the Blog.*)

The Webster says: The more people we enroll and connect with one another, the more powerful we each become.

7. Bianchini's Law of Viral Loops:

"When your currency is ideas, people become emotionally attached. Then you become a public utility like Blogger, YouTube, or Facebook." (Source: http://www.fastcompany.com/magazine/125/nings -infinite-ambition.html?page=0%2C2)

The Webster says: Your currency is ideas.

8. Trippi's Law:

"If you pay attention to the community you're building, then the community will step up and do the work."

The Webster says: The essence of the modern Web—and of developing the power to transform the world—resides in building community rather than broadcasting information.

9. Pariser's Law:

"This is not about us, it's about you."

The Webster says: Serve your community with humility.

10. Cage's Law:

"Begin anywhere."

The Webster says: It can appear daunting. When it does… just listen to John Cage, the greatest experimental composer of the 20th Century and a profoundly wise man: *begin anywhere.*

The end.

That's it.

You now know how to use the Web to transform the world.

Go do it.

There is only one final, optional, step to becoming an official member of the Noble Order of Websters. You must take The Webster's Oath: I WILL USE MY POWERS ONLY FOR GOOD. To take the oath, and get breaking news, now go to the homepage of TheWebstersDictionary.com, type in your name (or *nom de guerre*) and your email address, and just… click.

And one postscript...

About the Surgeon General's Warning on *The Websters' Dictionary*'s title page. Confession: *It actually wasn't issued by the actual Surgeon General.*

Apologies for this prank to Acting Surgeon General Rear Admiral Steven K. Galson, MD. (Um, shouldn't you be called the Surgeon *Admiral*, sir?)

Now that we've confessed, Admiral... please send that aircraft carrier group away from www.TheWebstersDictionary.com. It's scaring away the unique visitors. Sir.

APPENDIX A
SOME VALUABLE PLACES ON THE WEB

BOREDOM IS ALWAYS COUNTER-REVOLUTIONARY

www.theresistancearmy.com
The Official T-Shirt of The Noble Order of Websters.

THIS IS AN ANNOTATED bibliography of some amazingly useful sites that can help maximize the effectiveness of a policy or advocacy organization by providing access to useful information and low-cost tools. Think of it as a down payment on the Webster's Whole World Wide Web Catalogue. Meanwhile, come to TheWebstersDictionary.com, sign in at the Bar & Grill, and share your finds with your fellow Websters.

Wonderful open-secret sources of compiled information.

www.OpenSecrets.org: Who has given how much money to what candidates? What are the lobbyists being paid, and by whom?

www.Guidestar.com: Free access to information on 1.7 million nonprofits.

www.NetSol.com: Go to WHOIS to find out who owns a website and how to contact them (unless they have elected to keep it secret).

www.Quantcast.com: A new-media measurement service that enables advertisers to view audience reports for millions of sites and services to build their brands with confidence.

www.Alexa.com: Traffic rankings and an amazing blog at http://awis.blogspot.com.

www.SiteMeter.com: Comprehensive real-time website tracking and counter tools give you instant access to vital information about your site's audience.

www.wikipedia.org: A magnificent demonstration of the power of something very like "open source"—people collaborating to write an amazingly informative encyclopedia. By no means infallible, but then neither is the Britannica.

www.edventure.com: Esther Dyson, the Angel of the Internet, is believed to prefer that the Wikipedia be described as "peer-to-peer" rather than "open source." Dyson is one of the smartest people in the world of the Web. Thank Heaven she uses her powers only for Good, an inspiration to Websters everywhere. This is her website.

www.sourcewatch.org: A directory of the people, organizations, and issues shaping the public agenda. A primary purpose of SourceWatch is documenting the PR and propaganda activities of public relations firms and public relations professionals engaged in managing and manipulating public perception, opinion, and policy. SourceWatch also includes profiles on think tanks, industry-funded organizations, and industry-friendly experts that work to influence public opinion and public policy on behalf of corporations, governments, and special interests.

www.presidentialwatch08.com/index.php/map/: A map of the political blogosphere. Too amazing.

www.google.com: In addition to its search engine, Google offers the following useful features (just look at the little thin band at the top that you never look at and pick one, or click on "more" for more options, including "even more....");

- **Trends:** Compare the world's interest in your favorite topics. Enter up to five topics and see how often they've been searched on Google over time.

- **Alerts:** Get email updates of the latest relevant Google results (Web, news, etc.) based on your choice of query or topic.

- **Google Earth:** Explore the world from your computer.

www.snopes.com: Tracks online hoaxes.

blog.compete.com/election2008: An invaluable "Complete Election Coverage 2008" section that tracks campaign site traffic and demographics, as well as blog presence.

www.techpresident.com: A discerning watch on all things Web-powered in the presidential election campaign.

www.techcrunch.com: News and features about applications of interest to Websters.

Service Providers:

www.Elance.com: A place to post Web-based projects and get bids from around the world. NOTE: Caveat emptor!

www.Craigslist.com: Ditto.

THE WEBSTERS' DICTIONARY | 157

www.krop.com: A high-end (and more expensive) way to find, or at least seek, Web design talent.

www.Godaddy.com: A leading registrar where you can buy a domain name, inexpensively.

www.google.com: Google features in this category include:

- **Calendar:** Keep track of all the events in your life, coordinate schedules with friends and family, and find new things to do—all with one online calendar.

- **Gmail:** Fast, searchable email. Still using AOL or Hotmail? How 1998!

- **Docs:** Still saving your documents on your hard drive? Save them on Google's hard drives instead. You can edit them from anywhere and pick who has access.

capwiz.com/capwiznews/IDK/archive/index.html: If you wish to make it simple for your community to send emails to their legislators, Capwiz, recent purchased by The Roll Call Group, a subsidiary of The Economist Group, is the market leader.

www.streamsend.com: Want a provider to let you send lots of emails at very modest cost? Streamsend has good references.

www.Blackbaud.com and www.Kintera.com: Donor management utilities. (There are many others.)

Dressing up your site:

www.creativecommons.org: An elegant intellectual revolution that permits users to use, with modest restrictions and no red tape, images and other content from many different sources on the Web. Simply indispensable.

www.sproutbuilder.com: A quick and easy way for anyone to build, publish, and manage widgets, mini-sites, mashups, banners, and more.

www.rovion.com: An amazing visual that embeds a little video of a person right into your site. Visually charming.

www.sitepal.com: An animated reader. Less charming but more versatile than rovion.

www.flickr.com/creativecommons: Millions of photos, searchable by subject, that you are authorized to use without red tape or cost. Just follow the license's rules.

www.ning.com and www.kickapps.com: Create your own social network easily and inexpensively (or even free).

www.qik.com: Upload cell phone videos to the Web in real time. Amaze your friends.

www.blipback.com: Similar to www.qik.com, only better, according to Knox Bronson, who is almost never wrong.

www.widgetbox.com: Don't know what a widget is? You'll be glad you went here and looked.

www.rockyou.com: The best slideshow ever!

www.snap.com: Contextual content. Lets your hyperlink take you to a snapshot of the linked site. Ultra cool. Concept stolen by the Webster from epolitics.com.

services.alphaworks.ibm.com/manyeyes/home: "Users can upload the data they want to visualize, then try sophisticated tools to generate interactive displays." – N.Y. Times

For breaking news of the Web advocacy sector:

www.TheWebstersDictionary.com: Be sure to sign up for the free All Points Bulletin, and, if you'd like to meet other Websters (united we stand and all that) go to the Bar & Grill, our own social network, and join.

www.TheNextRight.com: If you aren't reading Ruffini, Dayton, Henke, and company, you are not in the Know.

www.epolitics.com: Colin Delany, Threat or Menace? You decide. Whichever, he's totally in the sweet spot of the Web.

www.wired.com: It's not about the Web advocacy sector. It's about technology, with a special emphasis on the Web. Not all Wired readers are Websters, but all true Websters read Wired.

Security:

http://www.schneier.com: Your website is vulnerable in more ways than you dream. You can't really afford fully to secure it. But 130,000 people subscribe to the newsletter of Bruce Schneier, the Dirty Harry of the Internet. Good to know he's out there.

Michael Dobson

*P*ROJECT MANAGEMENT IS A *distinct specialty that identifies and allows you to clearly think through and follow the steps toward getting a job done according to the three great constraints of time, quality and cost. Michael Dobson, whose book* Practical Project Management *is* *widely hailed as a classic in the field, has generously provided the following chapter adapting the classical principles of project management to the task of developing a website. —Editor*

Website Project Management

By Michael Singer Dobson, PMP

Michael Dobson (http://www.dobsonsolutions.com) is the author of six books on project management. The American Eagle Group resource website describes his book Practical Project Management *as "Frankly, the best book on project management I have ever read." He pioneered multiple project management in his groundbreaking PMI book* The Juggler's Guide to Managing Multiple Projects, *and developed modern Triple Constraints theory in* Six Dimensions of Project Management. Library Journal *named his book* Enlightened Office Politics *(with Deborah Singer Dobson) as one of the top business books of 2001. He helped build the Smithsonian's National Air and Space Museum, managed creative operations for a leading game company, and has consulted and trained internationally for over 250 leading organizations.*

The formal project management process is a highly developed, standardized, and validated approach that allows people managing projects in very disparate fields to approach the complex management issues involved in a way that is both systematic and effective. However, the full-blown formal approach is overkill for most Web projects. Project management carries an overhead cost, and must therefore be tailored to the size, complexity, and risks of a given category of projects. In this overview, we'll take a bare-bones approach to the essentials of project management to get something appropriate for most Web projects. If your project is huge or particularly challenging, you may want to take a more rigorous approach. Even so, this brief overview will help you when it comes time to go into more detail about how projects work.

So, how complicated should we get?

Project management complexity and difficulty should be thought of separately from technical complexity and difficulty. Work can be enormously complex and difficult from a technical perspective and yet be relatively straightforward from a project management perspective, or vice versa. Web work often has significant technical complexity, but the project elements are usually pretty straightforward.

Is project management scheduling software, such as Microsoft Project®, necessary or appropriate? If your website program is at any given moment running thirty projects scheduled over a staff of twenty people, with multiple deliverables and numerous tasks per project, you may find that using software and even employing a full-time scheduler will improve your operation sufficiently to warrant the substantial costs involved. If, on the other hand, you're looking at one or two projects at a time, scheduled across three people, with six or seven work packages per project, graph paper and sticky notes are more appropriate technology. One size definitely doesn't fit all.

The Project Life Cycle

There are five steps in the standard project lifecycle. We'll explore each of these in turn.

1. **Project Initiation.** During project initiation, the project manager and team determine the preliminary scope of the project.

2. **Planning.** Planning involves identifying and scheduling the work packages or activities necessary to perform the work; constructing estimates of duration, cost, and resources; developing plans to ensure quality, manage risks, and control scope; establishing communications and reporting strategies; acquiring resources, both people and contracts; and integrating these elements into a comprehensive planning document.

3. **Execution.** Project execution involves acquiring and building the project team, performing the work, and producing deliverables.

4. **Monitoring and Control.** Project monitoring and control tracks conformance to plan, identifies discrepancies, handles change management, and provides feedback to update and progressively elaborate the plan.

5. **Closeout.** Finally, during project closeout, the project team transfers deliverables to the next stage. This sometimes involves turning them over to customers or users, and other times involves

operating or using the deliverables themselves. Either way, the project is completed, and the remaining work of the project team involves releasing resources to other projects, developing lessons learned for future improvement, and closing out the administrative elements of the project.

Project Initiation

Project initiation is the phase of the project cycle in which the project is defined and established. This process may be extremely formal or comparatively casual, but at some point on the road from "We're just talking about maybe doing something at some point" to "Yes, we have a project: why aren't you done yet?" you need a signpost: "You are now entering Project Land." Some project managers would add a second sign, "Abandon hope, all ye who enter here," but that's what you get in the absence of the five project essentials.

Make sure you, the client, and the team have a common and realistic understanding of what needs to be done. Use the questions in Table 1 to shape the process.

Table 1. Defining the initial project space. In moving from problem to project, a number of questions require answers.

Is there a problem?	Is this website adequate? Is it currently accomplishing what it should?
What is the problem?	Is it a design problem, a content problem, a methodology problem, a marketing problem, or a technical problem?
Is it in our jurisdiction?	Is it our website? Is someone else in charge of it? Do we have any business making changes?

Is it within our capabilities and expertise?	Do we have the knowledge? Do we have the skills? Can we take on this workload?
Does the client want us to solve the problem?	Does the client trust us? Is there a benefit to the client or other key stakeholders for keeping the problem alive rather than solving it? Does the client believe we have the capabilities and experience to solve this problem?
Is there funding to solve the problem?	Do we have the resources in our budget? Is the client expected to pay us to perform the necessary service? Is the price affordable, competitive, and proportionate?
Should we accept this assignment?	What are the consequences for us, both positive and negative, in taking on this project? If the financial consequences are not attractive, are there long-term considerations that should influence our decision? Is the decision in our hands, or is it made by our organizational superiors?
Should we do this work in-house or contract it?	Is it faster, cheaper, or better to choose one option over the other?
To whom should we assign it?	Who has the capability, expertise, and capacity to take on the responsibility for managing this project? Can we supply the necessary management support to someone who may not have all the desired qualifications?

The Triple Constraints

Because projects must always end, they are constrained in ways that don't necessarily apply to operations work. The project environment is bounded by the Triple Constraints of time, cost, and performance:

- **Time Constraint.** How long do we have? The time constraint can be expressed as a specific deadline (before the end of the fiscal year), an event trigger (before the failure rate hits ten percent), or a degree of urgency ("I need it yesterday!").

- **Cost Constraint.** How much can we spend? The cost constraint can be expressed as an amount of money, a number of person-hours, use of equipment, consumption of supplies, or intangibles (political capital, goodwill).

- **Performance Criteria.** What does the product have to do? Performance criteria can be expressed as functional and technical requirements, the project's purpose or desired end state, evaluation criteria, or the establishment of the "good enough" point.

The three dimensions of the Triple Constraint exist in a hierarchy, based on the particular priorities or goals of the project, known as Driver/Middle/Weak Constraint.

Let's imagine you need to produce a website to mobilize support for your position on an upcoming election. Time is usually the driver: If you get the website up after the election, who cares how good it is or how cheaply you produced it? If you're trying to build a long-term grass roots initiative, the performance quality is the driver. It may be a good idea to spend more money or take more time to make sure it's right. If your organization is just getting off the ground and you need a website for credibility, with program detail to follow later, cost drives the project, followed by time. Performance can be improved or added later.

There are six possible hierarchies of constraints. Any order is possible. You've probably experienced situations in which cost considerations drive the project, with time pressure in the middle, and performance the weak constraint. Even if performance is the weak constraint, there's still a minimum acceptable level of performance you must meet (just as in the previous example there's a maximum cost allowed, even though it's more flexible than usual)—but it may not be possible to achieve much more than the minimum.

To determine the right hierarchy of constraints, you have to understand the underlying "why" of the project. Notice in each of the examples that the "why" is clear. The hierarchy flows logically and necessarily. Sometimes you have to do some detective work, especially if there's conflict among your customers about the most important reason for the project.

You've got to get this right, however, because the requirements you develop and the strategy you pursue must reflect the right order of the constraints. Failure means an unhappy customer and an unsuccessful project.

Project Charter

The project charter is the piece of paper that marks the official beginning of the project. Before the project charter, the project is potential; afterward, the project is real. The least important characteristic of the project charter is that it contain the words "project charter" in the document. Perhaps a signed contract or a memo from the customer may be sufficient. A handshake or oral commitment is, however, insufficient, and opens you, your project, and your organization up to major potential risks. If your organization does not provide you with some documentation to certify that a project commitment actually exists, you should at a minimum confirm any oral understanding or handshake in writing yourself.

Project Planning

The transition between project initiation and project planning tends to be inexact. Sometimes the analysis of user needs and the preparation of functional and technical requirements are performed completely before the project is accepted and a project charter (or contract) issued. Other times, only a preliminary problem identification is made before the work becomes a project. The project manager and project team, along with the customer and user, must then perform the detailed analysis of user needs and requirements as part of the work of the project. In the first case, formal planning can start as soon as the project is established. In the second, planning becomes more of a process of discovery, and neither the customer nor the project team quite knows at the beginning what it will take to accomplish the project.

Don't confuse planning with scheduling. A schedule is, of course, an important element of any plan, but the plan doesn't end there. A project plan must take into account resources, risks, quality, communication, procurement, and many other areas of the project. It must provide a map and a blueprint of what the project is, how it will be done, who will do it (and with what resources), how problems will be addressed, how progress will be reported, and how the project team will interact with the customer, the performing organization, and other stakeholders.

Statement of Work

As noted, sometimes all user needs and requirements are developed prior to accepting the project. Other times, only a preliminary project scope has been established, and the project manager/project team must develop the full scope of work.

The Statement of Work is a narrative summary of the project, with the detailed project requirements forming a supplement. If it hasn't already been developed, now is the time. It's essential that all key stakeholders agree to the Statement of Work before the project moves forward. Failure to get agreement opens the project up to significant risks from miscommunication and misunderstandings.

A Statement of Work should be short and clearly written. When there are numerous details, develop those in a requirements format, using numbered statements organized by category.

Work Breakdown Structure (WBS)

Although the Statement of Work is essential to ensure agreement among key stakeholders about the scope and objectives of the project, more detail is needed to enable the project team to manage the project. The Work Breakdown Structure, commonly known simply as a WBS, uses a graphic approach to organize project scope and break the scope into manageable work packages. For each work package, the project team will develop estimates for duration and resource usage, identify risks, assign responsibilities, and develop the other important project management tools.

Think of the WBS as the foundation and framing of a house. Even though the foundation and framing of the house is not very visible in the final construction, it's clear that the quality of the house will surely be no better than the quality of the house will surely be no better than the quality of the foundation and framing. The quality of your overall plan cannot be better than the quality of the WBS that underlies the other planning elements.

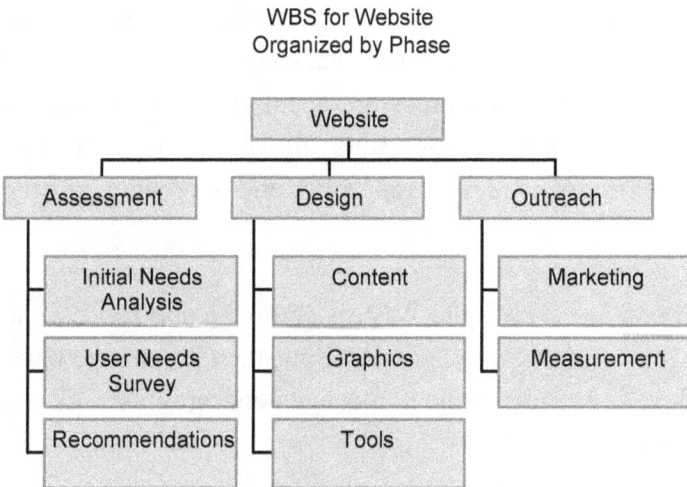

WBS for Website
Organized by Phase

```
                    ┌──────────────┐
                    │   Website    │
                    └──────────────┘
        ┌───────────────┼───────────────┐
┌──────────────┐ ┌──────────────┐ ┌──────────────┐
│  Assessment  │ │    Design    │ │   Outreach   │
└──────────────┘ └──────────────┘ └──────────────┘
   ┌──────────────┐  ┌──────────────┐  ┌──────────────┐
   │ Initial Needs│  │   Content    │  │  Marketing   │
   │   Analysis   │  └──────────────┘  └──────────────┘
   └──────────────┘  ┌──────────────┐  ┌──────────────┐
   ┌──────────────┐  │   Graphics   │  │ Measurement  │
   │  User Needs  │  └──────────────┘  └──────────────┘
   │    Survey    │  ┌──────────────┐
   └──────────────┘  │    Tools     │
   ┌──────────────┐  └──────────────┘
   │Recommendations│
   └──────────────┘
```

Figure 1. Work Breakdown Structure. The WBS organizes and defines the scope of the project and serves as the underpinning of the other planning tools. The better the quality of the WBS, the better the quality of subsequent steps in the planning process. This WBS is displayed in "org chart" format; you will also see the WBS presented in outline form. Use sticky notes on a whiteboard or flip chart to create the WBS so you and your team can work collaboratively and explore different options.

Develop the WBS using sticky notes on a whiteboard or flip chart, rather than by using project management software. Although project management software has numerous advantages that increase along with the size of your project, the software is generally not conducive to group brainstorming. It's important to stay flexible and explore different options for laying out the project.

Sticky notes with subordinate activities are known as "control accounts," and they represent the management and organizational structure of the project. Sticky notes without subordinate activities are "work packages." It is at the work package level that resources are spent and project work is accomplished. Control accounts allow you to "roll up" information to facilitate reporting and oversight of the project.

When you are certain the WBS is complete and reflects the management structure you will follow, then it's time to enter the data into your project management program, if you choose to use one.

You will normally have to develop the information for this sheet piecemeal. At the beginning of the process, you may only be able to identify the names of the individual work packages. Due dates, WBS numbers, detailed work descriptions, and other information is added as it is developed. To save time and improve performance, consider having the team members who will perform each task do most of the work of developing the form (subject to project management approval, of course) and recycle task information sheets from previous projects.

Schedule Development

Two scheduling tools are common in project management: the Gantt chart, which is essentially a bar graph over a calendar; and the network diagram, which shows the sequence in which activities will be performed. For small and medium-sized projects, the Gantt chart is the most common and easiest scheduling tool; for very large projects, the network diagram is more appropriate.

Even when the Gantt chart will be used as the scheduling tool, it's often better to lay out project activities and work packages as a network diagram first, then convert the information to the Gantt chart format. Here's how to develop both tools.

Network Diagram

A network diagram resembles a computer flow chart. To build a network diagram, use the "work package" sticky notes from your WBS. Do not use any "control account" sticky notes in making the network diagram.

The first step is to create a "Start" milestone for your project. A milestone is a work package that has zero duration and no associated work or resource consumption. In other words, a milestone is simply a signpost. Traditionally, a milestone is represented by the shape of a diamond. Turn a sticky note 45° to indicate that a given work package is a milestone.

Next, lay out the subsequent work packages in the order they are to be performed. Activities can be *dependent* (following a predecessor activity) or *parallel* (performed at the same time as other project activities). Dependent activities are sometimes required by the logic of the work (i.e., you can't upload a website before it's developed), and are sometimes driven by resources or other factors (i.e., the same person can produce the graphics and write the content, but not at the same time). If no particular order is demanded by logic, you can choose whichever order you prefer.

When all activities have been placed and connecting lines drawn, create a "Finish" milestone. Connect all unlinked activities to Finish so that every work package has at least one predecessor and at least one dependent activity—don't leave any orphaned work packages.

Normally, more than one sequence of activities is possible. As with the WBS, the correct order for your project is the one that represents how you and your team plan to approach this project.

Figure 2 shows a sample network diagram.

Sample Network Diagram

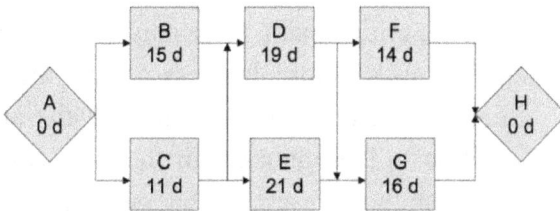

Figure 2. Network Diagram. This network diagram reflects the order in which work packages will be performed. Note that estimated durations have been assigned to each activity.

Here's how to read the network diagram. Task A is a milestone and serves as the start of the project. Both tasks B and C are dependent on the start milestone. Task D is dependent on both tasks B and C; task E is dependent only on task C. Task F is dependent on task D; task G is dependent on both tasks D and E. Task H, the finish milestone, is dependent on both tasks F and G.

So, how long will the project take? With dependency relationships crossing from top to bottom and back again, the answer takes a little bit of calculation. You need to find the longest path through the project network to determine the length of the project. The longest path is commonly known as the *critical path.* If you use project management software, it will determine the critical path for you automatically. You can do it manually by performing a "forward and backward pass," but that's beyond our scope.

Do a Web search for "forward and backward pass" and you'll find all the instructions you need.

If a task isn't on the critical path, there may be *float,* or extra time to finish the task before lateness affects the project deadline. Figure 4 shows the critical path and the availability of float. (The numbers in the four corners of each task come from the forward and backward pass.)

Critical Path and Float

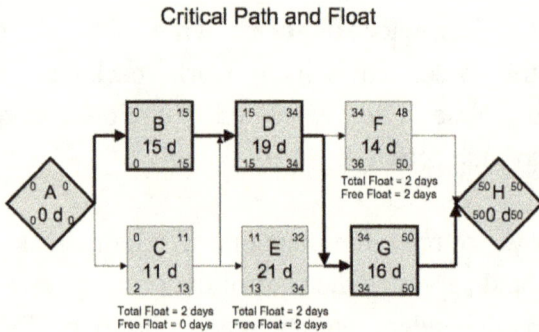

Figure 3. Critical Path and Float. A task is *critical* if any delay in the activity results in a delayed finish of the project. A task can have delay equal to its float without affecting the project's deadline. *Free float* is the amount of delay before the task forces a delay in any subsequent activity; float that is not free is *shared* with other activities. Activities C and E, for example, each have two days of total float, but the float in Activity C isn't "free," it's shared with Activity E.

Gantt Chart

The network diagram allows you to design the sequence of activities, but it's not a very intuitive way to visualize how long the project will take. For that, the Gantt chart is much clearer. A Gantt chart is essentially a bar graph of the schedule in calendar time. Almost all project management software will display a Gantt chart easily, but you can use graph paper or a spreadsheet program if you don't have a need for specialized project management software. Figure 4 shows the network diagram converted to a Gantt chart (this one done in Microsoft Excel®).

Gantt charts help you assign resources, track progress, and in a multiple-project environment, oversee the progress of all projects simultaneously. You can identify how resources are used across multiple project boundaries, and even compare different versions of the same project side by side.

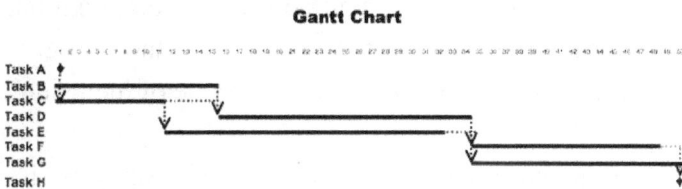

Figure 4. Gantt chart. The Gantt chart displays the schedule as a bar graph over time. It is the easiest schedule to develop and can be read by people without formal project management training.

Risk Management Planning

Because projects are temporary and unique, risks are inherently part of project management. A risk differs from a problem in tense: problems are present tense; risks are future tense. Every risk in your project will eventually go away—some by not happening at all, and others by turning into problems.

Risks include threats (negative risk events) and opportunities (positive risk events). While threat avoidance and threat management normally occupy the majority of a project manager's focus, it's worth it to spend some time on opportunities as well.

Here are the steps in risk management:

1. *Risk identification.* Through brainstorming, review of lessons learned on previous projects, and analysis of project documentation (requirements, user needs, terminal objectives, contracts, etc.), compile a list of potential risks for the project. In the initial risk identification process, err on the side of inclusion.

2. *Risk analysis.* The goal of risk analysis is to understand each risk thoroughly, prioritize the risks, and identify those risks that most require attention on the part of the project manager and project team.

3. *Risk response planning.* When your risks have been identified and analyzed, it's time to figure out what you plan to do about them. There are a limited number of available strategies for managing threats and opportunities on your project. Consider all possibilities before making your final decision.

When determining which strategy to follow, you need to look at two additional issues: *residual risk* and *secondary risk.* Residual risk is the risk left over after you've applied your risk response strategy. Secondary risk is new risk created by your proposed solution. Use Table 2 to determine your risk response options and consequences.

Strategy	Description	Residual Risk?	Secondary Risk?
Avoidance (Threat)	Change the project so that the risk event cannot occur, or the project is completely protected from its consequences.	No	Yes
Transfer (Threat)	Give the risk to another party. Financial risk is often transferred using insurance or contracting. Management risk can be transferred to other departments or other managers, as appropriate.	Yes	Yes

Mitigation (Threat)	Reduce the threat by lowering its likelihood of occurrence or by lowering its impact on project objectives	Yes	Yes
Exploitation (Opportunity)	Use the opportunity to improve the project's timeliness, cost, or quality.	Yes	Yes
Enhancement (Opportunity)	Try to improve the opportunity's probability or impact.	Yes	Yes
Sharing (Opportunity)	Transfer the opportunity elsewhere, such as to another project.	Yes	Yes
Active Acceptance (Either)	Develop a contingency plan to be triggered if the risk occurs or if it appears immediately likely to occur.	Yes	Yes
Passive Acceptance (Either)	Do nothing unless the risk occurs, then figure out a strategy based on the facts at hand.	Yes	No

Table 2. Risk Response Options. There are a limited number of potential risk responses for threats and opportunities, shown in the following grid. Note that the

potential for residual and secondary risk is almost always present.

Project Execution

In a way, all the earlier sections of this chapter serve as a guide to project execution. Project execution is performing the work of the project, and as a result it is necessarily tailored to the unique environment of that project.

From the project manager's perspective, there are a few elements that involve classical project management activities. First is quality assurance. Second is acquiring, development, and leading the project team. Third is managing any associated contracts. Fourth, the project manager must keep stakeholders informed.

Project Monitoring and Control

Project monitoring and control includes all the oversight issues necessary to oversee the project. These activities divide into two groups: monitoring project progress in the areas of time, cost, and performance; and dealing with changes to the project, both voluntary and involuntary.

Such activities as status meetings, progress reports, and review of work performed to date give the project manager information about the progress of the project. You need to establish in advance how and when you will be gathering this information.

Discrepancies between the plan and your project reality result in involuntary change: The project schedule is slipping, costs are increasing, and performance is not meeting expectations. (Or, if you're lucky, the project is early, requires fewer resources than you expected, and the results are much better than anticipated.) Minor discrepancies may not require action on your part, but any large discrepancy requires investigation.

The final part of risk management takes place during this phase: risk monitoring and control. You may find that risks you thought likely and serious turn out to be unlikely and minor, while other risks climb the hit parade with alarming speed. Review and update your risk management plan periodically, and monitor how well your proposed risk strategies are working. Make changes as necessary.

Voluntary change occurs when stakeholders request or require you to make changes to the previously approved project scope. "Scope creep" is a traditional enemy of project success. Scope changes by themselves aren't the problem—unmanaged and undocumented scope changes are what you need to worry about.

A good change management system always requires that changes be made in writing, reviewed for project impact, then approved by the appropriate party (which may or may not be the project manager or even someone inside your own organization). The impact to the project of the proposed change is the critical issue. Does the change in scope affect the timeline, the resources required, or the quality of other project elements? Do you simply want to accept the impact (yes, it will take three more weeks, but that's okay) or in approving the change do you need to implement corrective action (three weeks delay is unacceptable, so the price of the contract must be increased to allow addition of one more staff member, or not all modules will be rolled out in the initial phase)?

Project Closeout

Projects are temporary; therefore, they must end. Ending the project is known as project closeout. In project closeout, the product of the project must be moved to the next phase (implemented, given to the customer, uploaded), any contracts must be completed, the project team and other resources must be assigned to new work or returned to the labor pool, final reports must be provided, and the project files must be completed and archived.

The two remaining steps in project closeout have more to do with future projects than with the current project, but they are no less important. First, you need to celebrate success. Even though the next project is calling, it's important to acknowledge the hard work and efforts that made the current project successful. Say thank you in a meaningful way: write a letter, prepare a certificate, throw a party, or take people to lunch.

The final step is developing lessons learned. Although you can't do continuous improvement within a project, you can definitely improve the way in which you perform future projects. To do that, you must extract the learning value from today's experience. Avoid allowing this to become a "blamestorming" session. It's no longer relevant who did what wrong. What's relevant is how future projects can be better.

Conclusion

Project management was originally developed for large industrial and engineering projects. To make it relevant and useful for smaller projects, we must be careful to scale our project management to the size of our projects and the risks and complexities we are likely to encounter.

If you haven't used formal project management techniques on previous projects, start small and add complexity and sophistication as appropriate. Don't be afraid to decide, after a fair trial, that a given technique may not deliver the project results you desire.

Projects are as old as human history, and the Triple Constraints of time, cost, and performance shape the universe of our work. Within that balance, you can do great things. Project management is a useful tool to get the most out of any situation.

www.ingramcontent.com/pod-product-compliance
Lightning Source LLC
Chambersburg PA
CBHW031509270326
41930CB00006B/327

* 9 7 8 0 9 8 2 0 7 5 6 1 6 *